THE QUILTED APPLE

by Laurene Sinema

That Patchwork Place®

Credits

Editor-in-Chief .... Barbara Weiland
Technical Editor .... Kerry I. Hoffman
Managing Editor .... Greg Sharp
Copy Editor .... Liz McGehee
Proofreader .... Tina Cook
Design Director .... Judy Petry
Text and Cover Designer .... Sandra Seligmiller
Production Coordinator .... Karin LaFramboise
Photographer .... Brent Kane
Illustrators .... André Samson
                                                  Sandra Seligmiller

Library of Congress Cataloging-in-Publication Data
Sinema, Laurene.
    The Quilted Apple / by Laurene Sinema.
       p.   cm.
    ISBN 1-56477-060-5 :
      1. Patchwork. 2. Quilting.   I. Title.
  TT835.S552   1994
  746.46 — dc20   94-20398
                           CIP

Acknowledgments

*Many thanks to all who generously shared their exper-
tise in:*

    the making of the quilts, pillows, and pincushions;
    computer and proofreading skills; and
    cooking and recipes.

And to:

    Nancy J. Martin of That Patchwork Place,
        who asked once and then again;
    The Quilted Apple staff, who faithfully
        tended the shop day after day;
    Janet Carruth, who has always been there as a
        friend and quilting partner;
    and Gerry, a husband who accepts totally.

MISSION STATEMENT

WE ARE DEDICATED TO PROVIDING QUALITY PRODUCTS THAT
ENCOURAGE CREATIVITY AND PROMOTE SELF-ESTEEM IN OUR
CUSTOMERS AND OUR EMPLOYEES.

WE STRIVE TO MAKE A DIFFERENCE IN THE LIVES WE TOUCH.

That Patchwork Place is an employee-owned, financially secure company.

The Quilted Apple's staff spices this appealing shop (left to right) Helen Ohlson, Ann Bevilockway, Heidi Eberenz, Laurene Sinema (shop owner), Shirley Weagant, Barbara Voita, and Lynda Brown. Ginger Sanchez-Loupe not pictured.

Contents

The first home of the Quilted Apple, a red barn, is now one of the village buildings featured in a series of miniature historical wooden buildings. *Cat's Meow Village©* is displayed here in an antique secretary.

HOW THE QUILTED APPLE CAME TO BE

The Shop

The Arizona Quilter's Guild was born in the spring of 1978. After months of research and preparation, Janet Carruth and I invited several quilters from around the state to lunch. At that table, on that day, an idea became a plan. Each attendee went home to spread the word to other quilters about the first annual meeting of "The Guild." More than seventy-five people attended the first annual meeting later that year. We elected officers and organized chapters throughout the state. I served as the first president.

Our interest in quiltmaking did not stop there. Janet and I researched quilt shops across the nation, from New York state to California. We inquired about the physical size of the shops, number of fabric bolts, classes, number of employees, and much more. Our plan was to open a quilt shop, and in September 1978, The Quilted Apple opened in a red barn on a busy Phoenix street. Thirteen bolts of fabric, tremendous courage, enthusiasm, exciting classes, and quiltmaking expertise greeted the first shoppers. Over the next five years, the number of students, customers, and staff grew. The barn was bursting from top to bottom with fabric, patterns, and books, and the parking was inadequate.

🍎 THE QUILTED APPLE

A rambling house with many rooms, huge trees, and ample parking became the second home of The Quilted Apple. For eight years, the staff, customers, and students delighted in the space and the ambiance of the new location. Then, it was time for another move.

In August 1991, the shop moved around the corner to its present location. Park benches in front of The Quilted Apple invite shoppers and their spouses to rest a moment or two. The shop's happy, warm atmosphere greets all who enter. Along with a large variety of quilting fabrics, you will find quiltmaking tools and books, antique furniture displaying boutique items, a corner for rug hooking, another for smocking, a children's reading area, and, of course, lots of quilts. Students and teachers enjoy the large, bright classroom. The Quilted Apple is the perfect home away from home for all quilters and quilt lovers.

Laurene Sinema

The Staff

Custom quilting is expertly done by staff members (left to right) Una Jarvis, Ruth Umble, and Lori Heikkila.

After six years, Janet left the partnership to be a full-time mother and homemaker. She continues to teach and plan tours, and during the three-day "birthday celebration," she greets old friends, customers, and students.

Shop manager Heidi Eberenz and the staff have a breakfast meeting every Wednesday morning. Shirley Weagant, Lynda Brown, Helen Ohlson, Barbara Voita, Heidi, and Laurene provide delicious meals. We discuss shop policies, set goals, solve problems, and plan classes. In addition, we share happy and sad events in our lives and those of our families.

Three times a year, the staff and teachers meet for dinner and review the class schedule for the next four months. We discuss each class and show samples. The evening gives each person a vested interest in all the classes.

The Quilted Apple Club is hosted by a member, in her home, on the third Thursday of each month. Forty talented people who are current or past employees or quilting teachers share delicious food, recipes, friendships, and their latest quilting projects. The club started shortly after The Quilted Apple opened, to give Janet, Laurene, and the staff an opportunity to share what they loved most—quilting and quilting ideas. Now, fifteen years later, the group and the talent have increased tenfold. Membership in the club is lifetime. Those who have moved away tell us there is nothing anywhere to compare with the Quilted Apple Club.

Valerie Bowman listens intently to one of Laurene's stories during Apple Day Club at The Quilted Apple.

Teacher Janet Carruth assists Sally Patterson with her project. The Apple Ruggers (a rug hooking club) meet on the third Wednesday of each month.

Other Happenings

Around September 22 each year, The Quilted Apple celebrates its birthday. For three days, it is our good fortune to greet friends—both old and new—share stories of families and health, and give hugs to those we would not have known without The Quilted Apple!

The first day of December brings with it a month of festivities at The Quilted Apple. Wreaths and garlands adorn windows and doors. The aroma of hot spiced cider permeates the air, and holiday music adds to the spirit of the season. A children's shop is filled with gifts for family and friends. Wish lists are presented by husbands and filled by the staff.

Janet coordinates tours for the shop employees and customers. Past tours include a visit to the Amish areas of Pennsylvania and quilt exhibits in Los Angeles, Santa Fe, and New York City. They have all been enjoyable and memorable.

Clubs abound at The Quilted Apple, and members become friends who cherish the opportunity to meet often. Inspiration and enthusiasm are the gifts of the day. Clubs include:

Masters Class: 1st Saturday of each month
Apple Day Club: 2nd Thursday of each month
Primitive Spirit: 3rd Friday of each month
Tat and Talk Club: 4th Monday of every other month
Primitive Doll Club (2 clubs): 2nd Wednesday and 4th
    Monday of every other month
Apple Ruggers (a rug hooking club): 3rd Wednesday
    of each month
Appliqué Lovers: 1st Saturday of each month

Our parent/child classes give mothers, fathers, and grandparents the opportunity to spend time with their children and grandchildren. Planning the projects for the young students is a challenge for the staff and teachers.

Custom quilting is an integral part of The Quilted Apple. Customers bring antique and new quilt tops to be hand quilted, repaired, or bound. In addition, quilts are designed, pieced, and quilted for customers. Una Jarvis, Ruth Umble, and Lori Heikkila work in their homes to complete the custom stitching. Helen Ohlson is our staff consultant who watches over these heartwarming tasks.

At least twice a year, The Quilted Apple hosts well-known teachers from across the nation. We schedule workshops, lectures, and fashion shows. This is wonderful for quiltmakers in our area who do not have an opportunity to travel to symposiums in other parts of the country.

Students, customers, and friends think of us when they see apples during their travels and bring us gifts from all over the world. One friend was stitching an apple quilt block while she was traveling on a train in China. After learning she was from Arizona, a fellow passenger asked if she knew of The Quilted Apple. The quilt world is truly small!

Apple Day Club members Annette Mahon (left) and Dorothy Herberg (right) practice their appliqué.

THE PROJECTS

Apples galore—a peck, a bushel, and more. Pick your favorite—we've included some of ours—quilts, rugs, pillows, pincushions, and recipes. When life gives you apples, make applesauce—or quilts!

Apple Days—School Days

Finished Quilt Size: 40" x 60"
Photo: page 48

Primitive folk-art appliqué, combined with plaids and stripes, is a favorite of many of the students and customers at The Quilted Apple. Our Primitive Spirit Club has twenty-six members and meets monthly to stitch and share ideas. I like the bird eating the apple. Which block is your favorite?

Materials
44"-wide fabric

3 yds. assorted plaids and stripes for background
    blocks
$1/4$ yd. gold plaid for sun center
$1^1/8$ yds. assorted plaids and checks for schoolhouse
$3/8$ yd. assorted plaids and stripes for basket
$1/3$ yd. blue plaid for bird
$2/3$ yd. brown plaid for tree trunk and branches
$1/4$ yd. green plaid for apple tree leaves
$3/8$ yd. green plaid for fence background
$1/4$ yd. brown plaid for fence
Assorted plaid and striped scraps for apples, stems,
    leaves, sun rays, bell, bird wing, and beak
$1/2$ yd. red plaid for inner border and binding
2 yds. total of 11 plaids for outer border
$1^7/8$ yds. for backing
45" x 60" piece of batting
1 skein of black embroidery floss
1 skein of green embroidery floss

Making the Blocks

Refer to the photo on page 48 for color ideas. Cut, piece, and appliqué the following blocks, using the templates on pages 13-17 and the pullout pattern insert. Make plastic templates, following the directions on page 84. Appliqué the pieces in the order indicated on the templates.

Sun Block

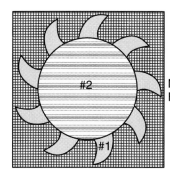

Make 1
Finished size: 13" x 13"

From assorted plaids and stripes for sun rays, cut:
    9 piece #1
From gold plaid, cut:
    1 piece #2
From background fabric, cut:
    1 square, $13^1/2$" x $13^1/2$"

Center the sun rays and sun center on the background block. Appliqué the rays first, then the center. Appliqué 1 block.

Schoolhouse Block

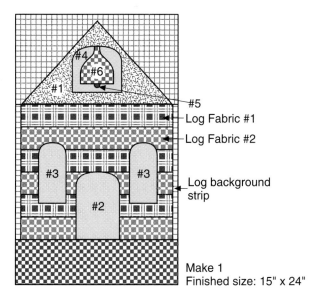

Make 1
Finished size: 15" x 24"

From assorted plaids and checks, cut:
    1 each of pieces #1–#6
    6 strips, each $13^1/2$" x $2^1/2$", for logs
    2 strips, each $1^1/2$" x $12^1/2$", for the log
        background
    1 rectangle, $15^1/2$" x $8^1/2$", for the roof
        background
    1 rectangle, $15^1/2$" x $4^1/2$", for ground

1. Alternate the 6 logs ($13^1/2$" x $2^1/2$" strips) and stitch them together. Stitch a $1^1/2$" x $12^1/2$" strip to each side of the log unit.
2. Center the roof (piece #1) on the background block, aligning the bottom edges. Appliqué the top 2 edges of the roof.
3. Stitch the roof unit to the top of the log unit.
4. Stitch the $15^1/2$" x $4^1/2$" rectangle to the bottom of the log unit.

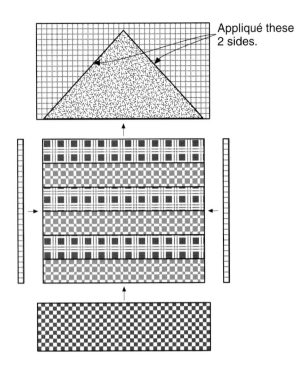

Appliqué these 2 sides.

5. Appliqué pieces #2–#6, in the numerical order indicated on the templates. Embroider the door and window details with an outline stitch, using 2 strands of black embroidery floss. Refer to the location on the templates. See "Embroidery Stitches" on page 87.

Basket of Apples Block

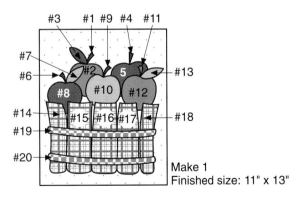

Make 1
Finished size: 11" x 13"

From assorted plaid and striped scraps, cut:
1 each of pieces #1–#13
From assorted plaids and stripes for basket, cut:
1 each of pieces #14–#20
From the background fabric, cut:
1 rectangle, 11½" x 13½"

Appliqué 1 block, using the templates and Appliqué Placement Guide on the pullout pattern insert.

Bird Block

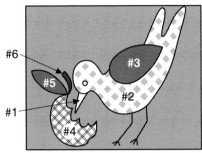

Make 1
Finished size:
15" x 12"

From blue plaid for bird, cut:
1 piece #2
From assorted plaid and striped scraps, cut:
1 each of pieces #1 and #3–#6
From background fabric, cut:
1 rectangle, 15½" x 12½"

Appliqué 1 block, using the templates and Appliqué Placement Guide on the pullout pattern insert. Embroider the bird legs and eye with an outline stitch, using 2 strands of black embroidery floss. Embroidery lines are indicated on the templates. See "Embroidery Stitches" on page 87.

Apple Blocks

Green Apple Block
Make 1
Finished size: 6" x 6"

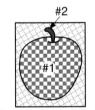

Orange Apple Block
Make 1
Finished size: 6" x 7"

Yellow Apple Block
Make 1
Finished size: 7" x 7"

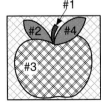

Red Apple Block
Make 1
Finished size: 7" x 8"

Yellow Apple
From assorted plaid and striped scraps, cut:
  1 each of pieces #1–#3
From background fabric, cut:
  1 square, 7½" x 7½"

Red Apple
From assorted plaid and striped scraps, cut:
  1 each of pieces #1–#4
From background fabric, cut:
  1 rectangle, 8½" x 7½"

Green Apple
From assorted plaid and striped scraps, cut:
  1 each of pieces #1–#3
From background fabric, cut:
  1 square, 6½" x 6½"

Orange Apple
From assorted plaid and striped scraps, cut:
  1 each of pieces #1 and #2
From background fabric, cut:
  1 rectangle, 6½" x 7½"

Appliqué 1 of each block, using the templates and Appliqué Placement Guide on the pullout pattern insert. On the orange apple, embroider the dimple with an outline stitch, using 2 strands of black embroidery floss. See "Embroidery Stitches" on page 87.

Fence Block

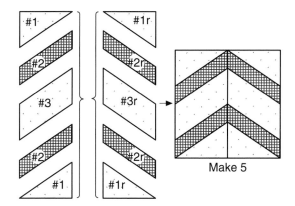

Make 5

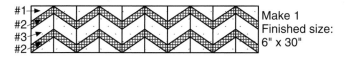

#1
#2
#3
#2
Make 1
Finished size:
6" x 30"

From green plaid for fence, cut:
  10 each of pieces #1 and #1r
  5 each of pieces #3 and #3r
From brown plaid for fence, cut:
  10 each of pieces #2 and #2r

Piece 1 block.

From scrap of red plaid, cut:
  1 apple from Fence block apple template

Apple Tree Background Block

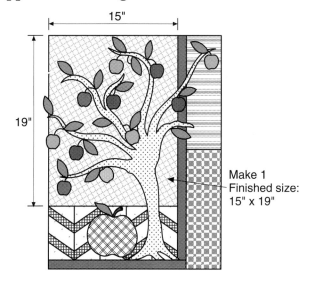

15"

19"

Make 1
Finished size:
15" x 19"

From background fabric, cut:
  1 rectangle, 15½" x 19½"

Assembling the Quilt Top

Use ¼"-wide seam allowances.
1. Referring to the Quilt Plan on page 8 and the quilt photo on page 48, sew all the blocks together.
2. For the inner border, cut 4 strips, each 1½" x 44". Join the strips, end to end. From the long strip, cut 2 strips, each 1½" x 50½", for the side borders and 2 strips, each 1½" x 32½", for the top and bottom borders. Sew the side borders to the quilt top, then the top and bottom borders. Press the seam allowances.

3. Measure through the center of the quilt and cut the border to that length each time you add a new border strip. To make the outer border, cut strips in random lengths, each 4$\frac{1}{2}$" wide. Sew them together, end to end. Sew the strips to the quilt, starting on the bottom and working clockwise around the quilt. Press.

4. Cut and appliqué in order the apple tree, apples, and leaves, following the Quilt Plan. The templates and Appliqué Placement Guide are on the pullout pattern insert. Piece dark brown checked fabric as needed to make the tree. Cut 11 apples and 16 leaves. Embroider the stems with a chain stitch, using 2 strands of green embroidery floss. See "Embroidery Stitches" on page 87.

5. Appliqué the apple in the Fence block, next to the apple tree, as shown on the Quilt Plan.

Finishing the Quilt

Layer the quilt top with batting and backing. Quilt as desired. Bind the edges. See "Quilt Finishing" on pages 89–93.

Mary's Fried Apples

"My father and mother had been married nearly fifty years when Mother passed away in March 1993. Mom's policy for my dad was: You stay out of my kitchen and I'll stay out of your garage! Dad didn't mind the policy since he enjoyed nearly everything Mom cooked. He did, however, teach her to make the fried apple dish that his mother made."

Mary Dyer, a teacher at The Quilted Apple, shares her recipe for fried apples. Mary has many quilting and fried-apple groupies!

> Salad oil (enough to coat the bottom of a large electric or stove-top skillet)
> 6 cups Jonathan apple slices
> 3 Tablespoons brown sugar
>
> Place apple slices in the oil-coated skillet and sprinkle brown sugar on top. Cover the skillet and fry the apples at medium high. Stir after 5 minutes. Cook 5 minutes more. The apples should be soft and juicy. Remove the cover and cook until lightly brown. Serve immediately. Serves 6.

◆

AN APPLE A DAY KEEPS THE DOCTOR AWAY!

—Anonymous

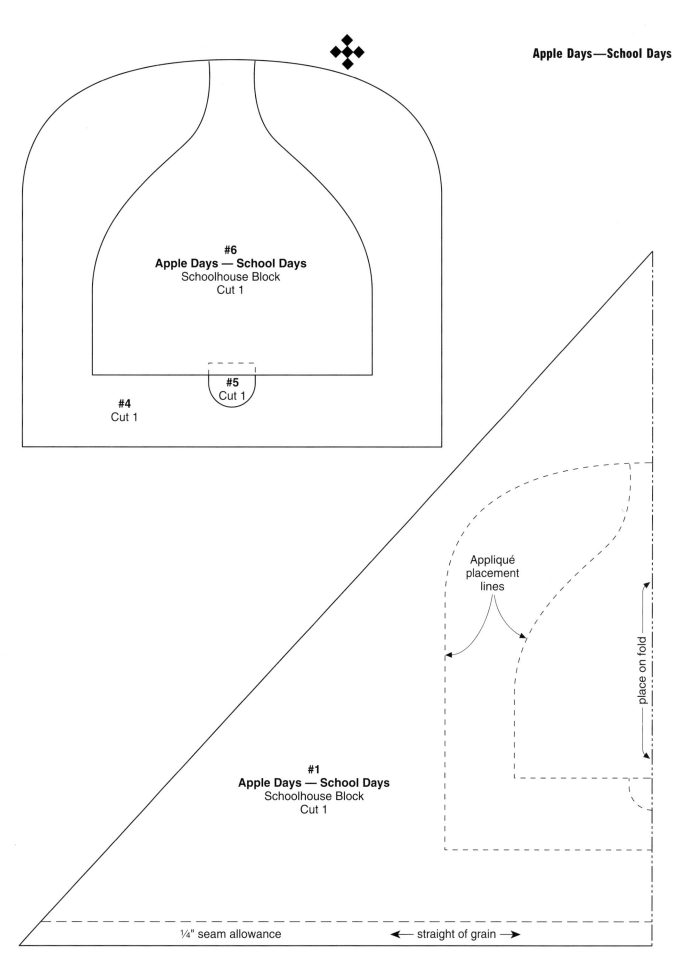

#6
Apple Days — School Days
Schoolhouse Block
Cut 1

#5
Cut 1

#4
Cut 1

Appliqué
placement
lines

place on fold

#1
Apple Days — School Days
Schoolhouse Block
Cut 1

¼" seam allowance

← straight of grain →

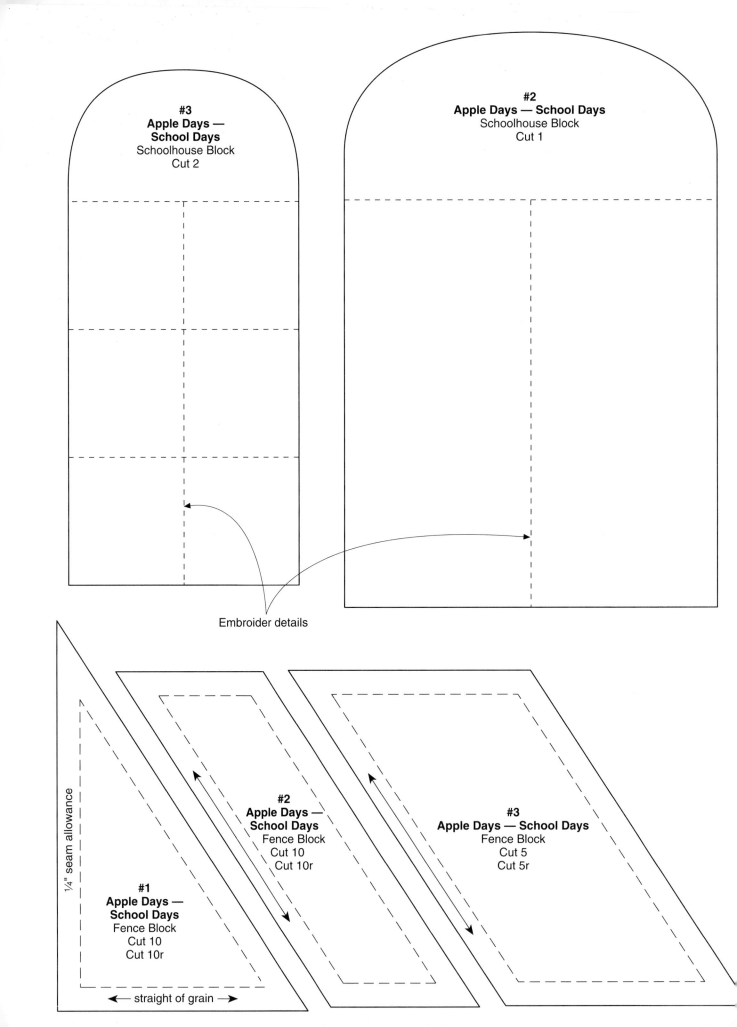

#3
Apple Days —
School Days
Schoolhouse Block
Cut 2

#2
Apple Days — School Days
Schoolhouse Block
Cut 1

Embroider details

¼" seam allowance

#1
Apple Days —
School Days
Fence Block
Cut 10
Cut 10r

#2
Apple Days —
School Days
Fence Block
Cut 10
Cut 10r

#3
Apple Days — School Days
Fence Block
Cut 5
Cut 5r

← straight of grain →

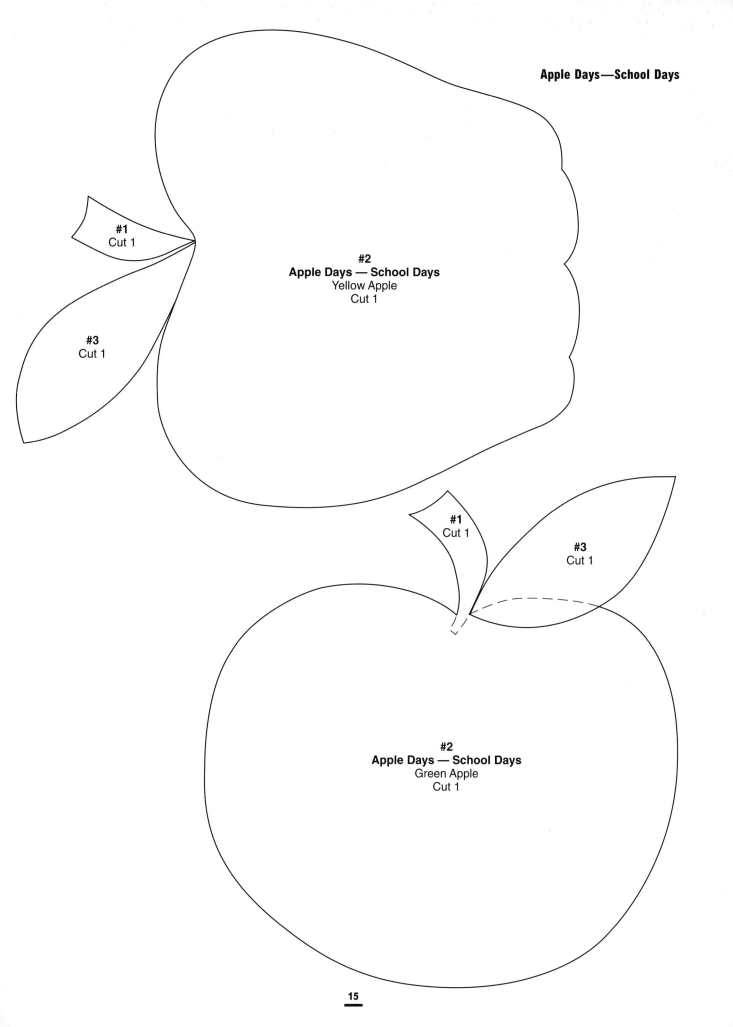

#1
Cut 1

#2
Apple Days — School Days
Yellow Apple
Cut 1

#3
Cut 1

#1
Cut 1

#3
Cut 1

#2
Apple Days — School Days
Green Apple
Cut 1

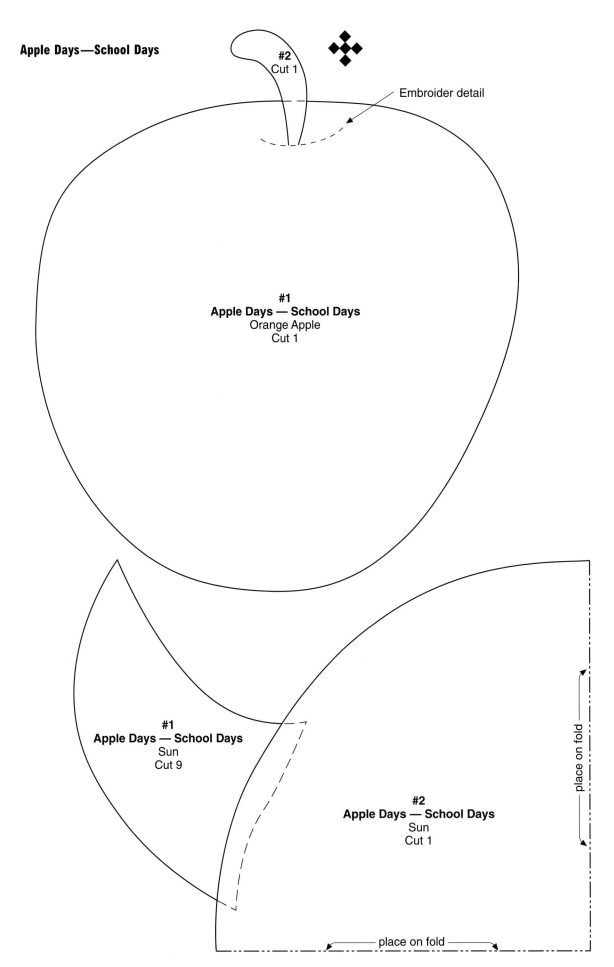

#2
Cut 1

Embroider detail

#1
Apple Days — School Days
Orange Apple
Cut 1

#1
Apple Days — School Days
Sun
Cut 9

#2
Apple Days — School Days
Sun
Cut 1

place on fold

place on fold

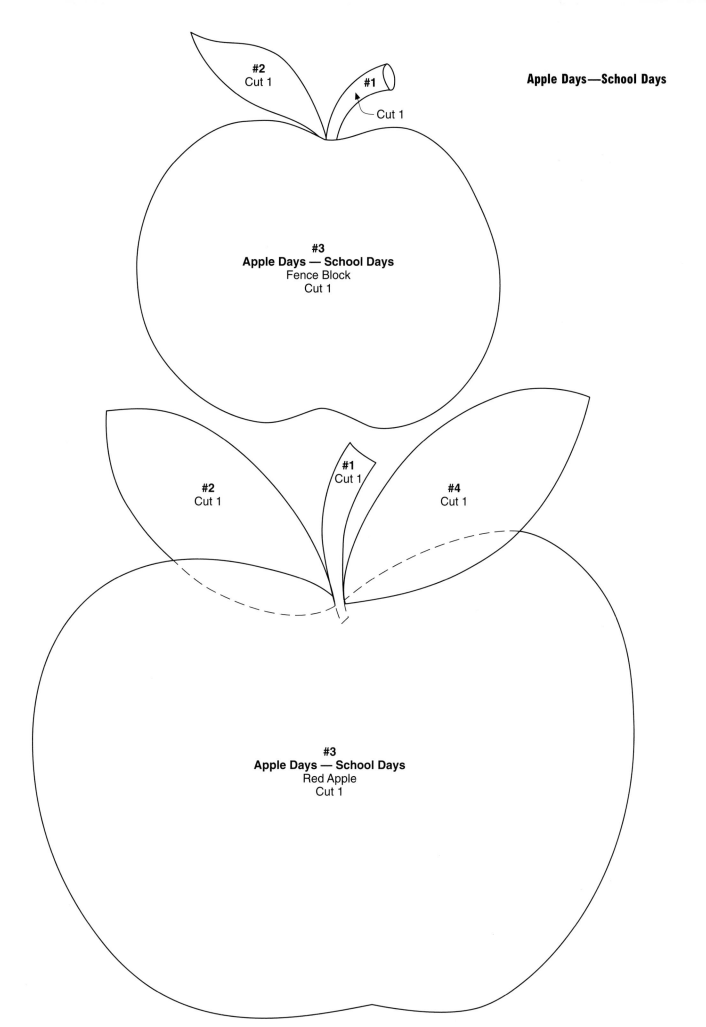

#2
Cut 1

#1
Cut 1

#3
Apple Days — School Days
Fence Block
Cut 1

#2
Cut 1

#1
Cut 1

#4
Cut 1

#3
Apple Days — School Days
Red Apple
Cut 1

Apple Harvesttime Table Rug

Finished Table Rug Size: 45" x 25"
Photo: page 48

In the midnineteenth century, wool penny rugs were used as decorative table covers. The large copper pennies of the time are thought to have been used as templates for the wool circles on the rugs. Different-sized circles were stacked upon each other, with the largest at the bottom and the smallest at the top. Each circle was embroidered with a buttonhole stitch, often in a contrasting color. Some of the rugs included appliquéd motifs.

This Harvesttime wool table rug was inspired by the penny rugs of yesteryear—with a few innovations. This rug gets prettier with each stitch you take. Due to the renewed interest in making hooked rugs, many beautiful hand-dyed wools are now available. They are rich in color and easy to work with.

Materials

60"-wide wool fabric (dense flannel)

32" x 40" black for background and borders
10" x 16" green for pine trees
3" x 6" blue for bird's body
3" x 3" red for bird's wing
3½" x 11" light gray for roof and chimney top
3" x 8" medium gray tweed for chimney and door
10½" x 12" dark gray for short logs
9" x 12" medium gray for long logs
3½" x 4½" yellow for window
4" x 10" black for door, window frames, and door-
    knob
7" x 10" each of 3 different greens for apple trees
9½" x 29" brown for apple tree trunks
10" x 10" red for apples
3" x 6½" beige for ladder
4" x 15" tan for bushel baskets
2" x 8½" light plaid for wagon
3" x 8" gray for wagon wheel and tongue
1 skein each of embroidery floss to match the
    appliqué pieces (or one shade darker)
6 skeins of tan embroidery floss for horseshoe border

Directions

Making the Foundation

1. Make plastic templates for the 2 horseshoe
   border shapes (Templates #1 and #2). Make
   freezer-paper templates for all the other motifs,
   following the directions on page 84. Do not
   add seam allowances. Use the templates on
   pages 21–22 and the pullout pattern insert.
2. From the black background fabric, cut:
   1 rectangle, 20" x 40", for the background
   2 strips, 2" x 20", for inside horseshoe border
       (sides)
   2 strips, 2" x 40", for inside horseshoe borders
       (top and bottom)
   2 strips, 3" x 18", for outside horseshoe border
       (sides)
   2 strips, 3" x 38", for outside horseshoe border
       (top and bottom)
   4 piece #2 for corner horseshoes
3. Mark each strip as directed below with a white
   marking pencil. Trim away the excess fabric
   outside the scallops.
   On each 2" x 20" strip, mark Template #1 side
       by side 8 times.
   On each 2" x 40" strip, mark Template #1 side
       by side 16 times.
   On each 3" x 18" strip, mark Template #2 side
       by side 7 times.
   On each 3" x 38" strip, mark Template #2 side
       by side 15 times.

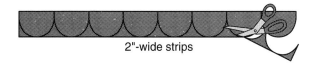

2"-wide strips

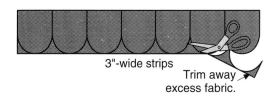

3"-wide strips

Trim away
excess fabric.

4. Place the inner border strips on the wrong side of the background rectangle as shown. Then place the outer border strips on top of the inner border strips. Match the placement line indicated on the border strips with the edges of the background. Pin the borders in place.

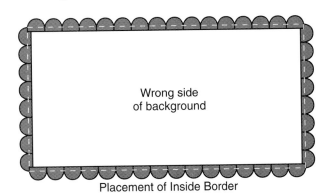

Placement of Inside Border

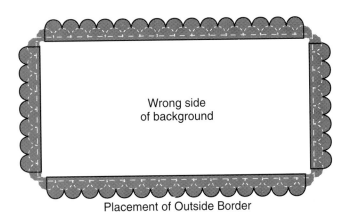

Placement of Outside Border

5. Place a corner horseshoe on each corner as shown. Pin.

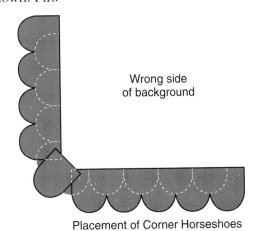

Placement of Corner Horseshoes

6. Machine stitch the borders in place by sewing 2 rows ¹/₄" apart. None of the motif or border edges are turned under.

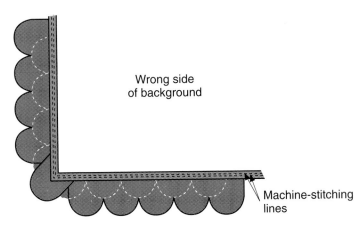

Appliqué Motifs

1. Pin all motifs in place, in the numerical order indicated on the templates, referring to the photo on page 48 and the Rug Plan on page 18 for location of the motifs. Use reverse appliqué for the window frame (piece #21). See "Reverse Appliqué Made Easy" on page 57.
2. Appliqué each motif in place with 2 strands of matching embroidery floss, using a buttonhole stitch (page 87).
3. Embroider the details of the baskets, tree branches, and wheel spokes with 2 strands of a darker shade of embroidery floss, using a running or an outline stitch (page 87).
4. Embroider around the edge of each border horseshoe with 6 strands of tan embroidery floss, using a buttonhole stitch. Refer to the photo on page 48.
5. To block the finished rug, place it wrong side up on your ironing board and press it with a damp cloth. Set your iron at the wool setting and use steam.

BUT I, WHEN I UNDRESS ME
EACH NIGHT, UPON MY KNEES
WILL ASK THE LORD TO BLESS ME
WITH APPLE-PIE AND CHEESE.

—Eugene Field
"Apple-Pie and Cheese"

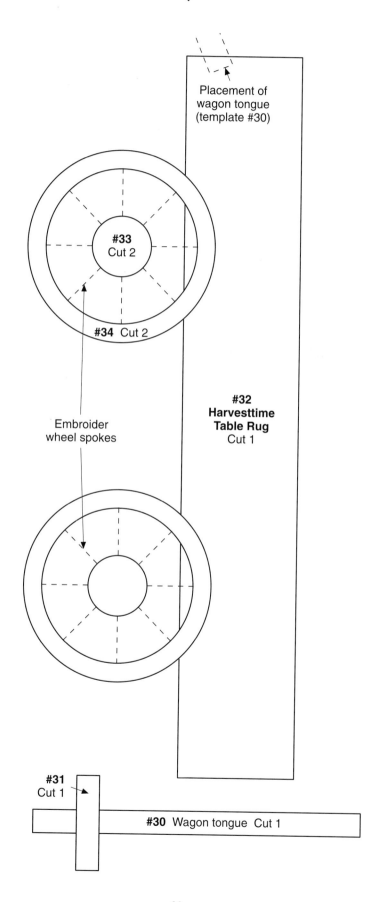

Placement of
wagon tongue
(template #30)

#33
Cut 2

#34 Cut 2

#32
Harvesttime
Table Rug
Cut 1

Embroider
wheel spokes

#31
Cut 1

#30 Wagon tongue Cut 1

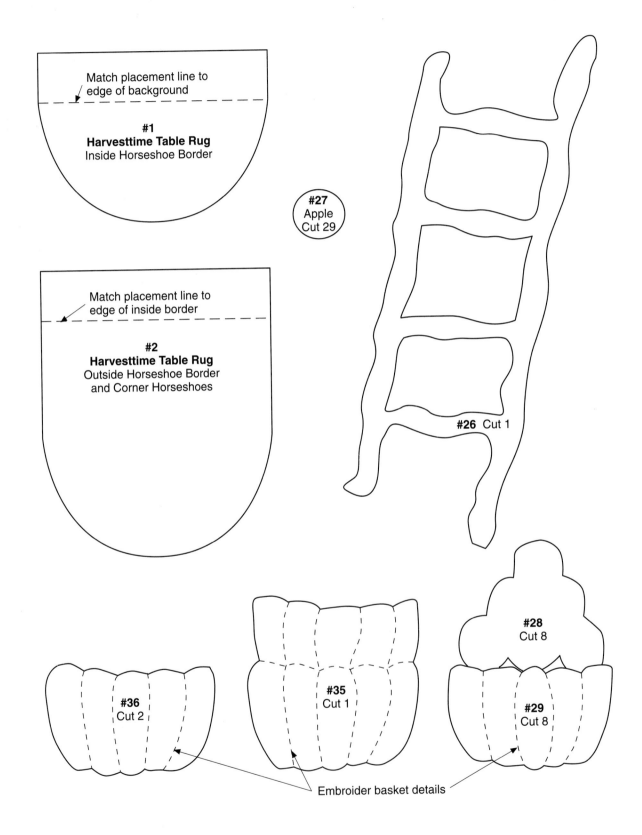

Match placement line to edge of background

#1
Harvesttime Table Rug
Inside Horseshoe Border

#27
Apple
Cut 29

Match placement line to edge of inside border

#2
Harvesttime Table Rug
Outside Horseshoe Border
and Corner Horseshoes

#26 Cut 1

#28
Cut 8

#36
Cut 2

#35
Cut 1

#29
Cut 8

Embroider basket details

An Album Apple

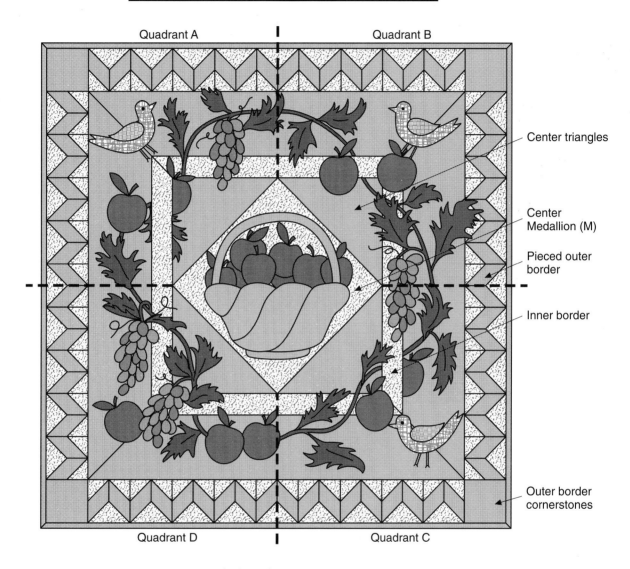

Quadrant A   Quadrant B

Center triangles

Center Medallion (M)

Pieced outer border

Inner border

Outer border cornerstones

Quadrant D   Quadrant C

Finished Quilt Size: 44" x 44"
Photo: page 46

Once a month, The Quilted Apple hosts the Masters Class. Its members are students who have completed a year-long series of Baltimore Album appliqué classes. Since 1989, over 200 members have shared their talents and enthusiasm for fine appliqué and have "graduated." Some have finished their album quilts and are planning new ones. Others are continuing to appliqué their first. Several have finished Folk Art Album quilts and miniature Baltimore Album quilts.

It is my good fortune to teach the hand appliqué classes. It's rewarding to see the progress students are making and the delight they take in new challenges.

Sometimes, new designs come to me at unusual times. This Basket of Apples design took form in the middle of the night when the house was quiet. I designed the border just as quickly. My first thought was: The Masters Class will love this. They do, and I hope you will also.

Materials

44"-wide fabric

1 yd. beige print for center block background and inner and outer borders

4 yds. beige solid for background, backing, and binding

1/2 yd. assorted purple solids, ranging from light to dark for grapes

1/2 yd. assorted red prints and solids for apples

1/4 yd. assorted blues for bird bodies

3 pieces gold, each 3" x 4 1/2", for bird wings

3/4 yd. dark green print for vine and leaves

1/2 yd. beige solid polished cotton for basket and handle

1/4 yd. dark beige print for basket trim

48" x 48" piece of batting

Cutting

From the beige print, cut:

1 square, 14 1/2" x 14 1/2", for the center medallion background

4 strips, each 2 1/2" x 25", for inner border

36 pieces from Outer Border Template #2

36 pieces from Outer Border Template #3

36 pieces from Outer Border Template #3 reversed

From the beige solid, cut:

2 squares, each 10 7/8" x 10 7/8"; cut once diagonally to yield 4 large center triangles

4 strips, each 6 1/2" x 36 1/2", for middle border

36 pieces from Outer Border Template #1

36 pieces from Outer Border Template #1 reversed

4 squares, each 4 1/2" x 4 1/2", for outer border cornerstones

2 strips, each 24" x 48", for backing

4 strips, each 1 1/2" x 47", for binding

From the dark green print, cut:

120" of 1 1/4"-wide bias strips for vine.

(See page 86.)

Directions

Use 1/4"-wide seam allowances for all pieced seams. Use the appliqué templates and Appliqué Placement Guide on page 27 and on the pullout pattern insert.

1. Make plastic templates for the birds and large apples (in the borders), following the directions on page 84. Make freezer-paper templates for the basket, center medallion apples (in the basket), and all the apple stems, leaves, and grapes. (See page 84.) Label each template with the location letter (M for medallion or quadrant A, B, C, or D) followed by the template number. The templates are on the pullout pattern insert.

2. Cut out all the appliqué pieces from the fabrics noted in the Materials list, adding scant 1/4"-wide seam allowances (3/16"). Label each piece. On basket pieces #20–#23, mark the intersection points a–f as indicated on the templates. These intersection points will help you align the basket pieces as you appliqué.

3. For the basket trim, cut enough 3/4"-wide bias strips from the beige print to make a 54" length. Fold the strip in half lengthwise with wrong sides together. Press.

4. With right sides together and raw edges aligned, sew the trim to each basket piece, stitching on the marked seam line of the basket piece. Stitch the trim onto each piece in the direction shown below. Press seam to the wrong side. Approximately 1/8" of the bias will show on the right side of the basket piece.

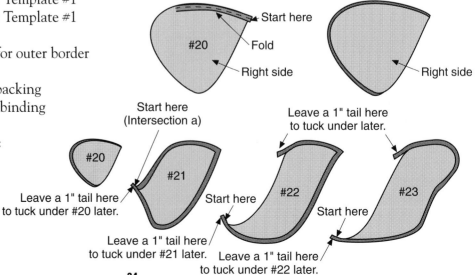

5. Sew basket pieces #20–#23 together, matching the intersection points a–f before stitching the basket to the background square.

6. To appliqué the center medallion, pin the basket, basket handle, apples, stems, and leaves to the background center square as indicated on the templates and Appliqué Placement Guide. Appliqué in place in numerical order as indicated on the templates.

7. Sew the 4 large corner triangles to the appliquéd center medallion. Press. (See page 88.)

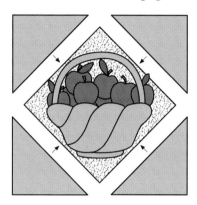

8. Sew the 2½"-wide inner border strips to the 6½"-wide inner border strips. Sew the border units to the medallion/triangle square, making mitered corners. (See pages 88–89.) Press.

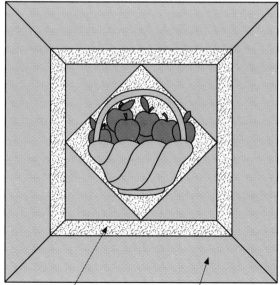

Beige print border   Solid beige border

9. Make ³⁄₈"-wide bias tube vines from the dark green 1¼"-wide bias strips. See "Making Stems and Vines" on pages 86–87 for making and appliquéing vines. Appliqué the vines in place in all 4 quadrants, opening the border seams where indicated to tuck in the end of the vine. In each quadrant, appliqué the remaining pieces in place in numerical order. Note that an apple in Quadrant A and in Quadrant C is tucked into the inner border seam. Do not appliqué the birds' tails and the portions of the leaves that overlap onto the pieced outer border at this time. You will complete the appliqué of these pieces later.

10. Piece 4 outer border units as shown. Stitch the parallelograms (Templates #1 and #1r) and the corner triangles (Template #3) together. Press. Next add the side triangles (Template #2). Sew 9 of the resulting units together to make 1 outer border unit. Make 4.

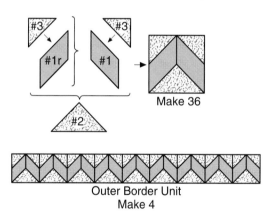

Outer Border Unit
Make 4

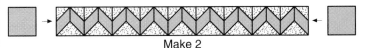

Tip

To insert the corner triangles, on the wrong side of the triangle, insert a pin in the corner of the triangle as shown, ¼" from the straight edges. Then insert a pin on the right side of the pieced parallelograms, ¼" from the inside corner.

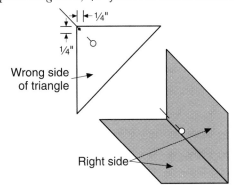

Match the point of the triangle to the point of the pieced parallelogram. The points should meet exactly. Pin triangle in place. Sew from the outer edge to the inside corner pin. Sew as close to the corner pin as possible without sewing past it.

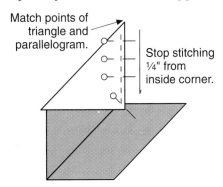

Pivot the remaining triangle point to match the remaining point of the parallelogram. Turn the pieces over and pin the triangle in place. Sew from the outer edge to the inside corner as you did before. Press.

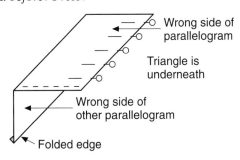

11. Stitch one 4½" corner square to each end of 2 of the outer border units. Press.

Make 2

12. Sew the 2 outer border units that do not have the corner squares to the top and bottom of the quilt top. Press.
13. Sew the remaining 2 outer border units to the sides of the quilt top. Press.
14. Complete the appliqué of the leaves and the birds' tails. Embroider the birds' eyes and legs and the grapevine tendrils using the outline stitch. (See page 87.)

Finishing the Quilt

Layer the quilt top with batting and backing. Quilt as desired or follow the quilting suggestion below. Bind the edges. See "Quilt Finishing" on pages 89–93.

Quilting Suggestions

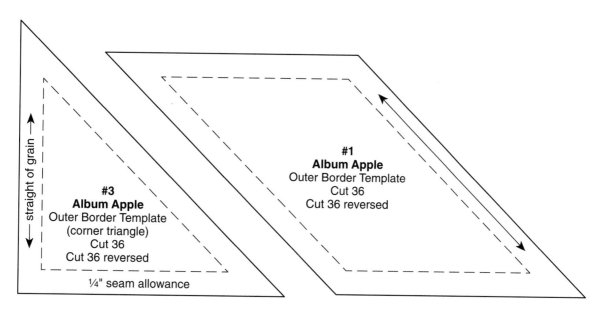

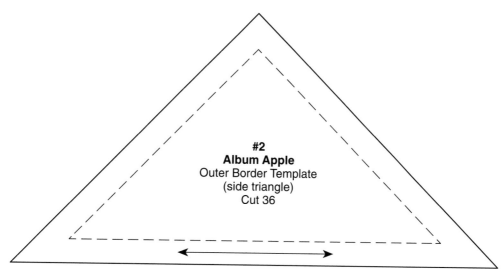

Love Apple

Finished Quilt Size: 60" x 60"
Photo: page 49

This nineteenth-century design is given a twentieth-century flavor by adding a Flying Geese border and border squares in many shades of red. Another name for the Love Apple block is Pomegranate block. Others identify the plant as a tomato. By any name, this bold, beautiful quilt is a joy to stitch.

Materials
44"-wide fabric

2¼ yds. off-white polished cotton
½ yd. beige for center block and border
¾ yd. green print for leaves
½ yd. brown for stem and vine
1 yd. red print for apples
¼ yd. gold print
1⅔ yds. assorted red prints for multiple-squares
    border
¾ yd. for binding
3¾ yds. for backing
64" x 64" piece of batting

Cutting

From the off-white polished cotton, cut:
    1 square, 18½" x 18½", for the center
    4 strips, each 8½" x 56½", for vine border

From the beige, cut:
    96 piece #7 for Flying Geese

From the green print, cut:
    48 piece #6 for Flying Geese
    89 piece #2 for leaves

From the brown, cut:
    1 piece #1 for center block stem
    3½ yds. of ⅝"-wide bias for vine (See page 86
      for making bias.)

From the red print, cut:
    4 strips, each 1½" x 20½", for inner border
    6 piece #4 for center block apples
    6 piece #4 reversed for center block apples
    3 piece #5 for center block apples
    8 piece #10 for vine border apples
    8 piece #10 reversed for vine border apples
    4 piece #11 for vine border apples
    8 piece #13 for vine border (corner) apples
    8 piece #13 reversed for vine border (corner)
      apples
    4 piece #14 for vine border (corner) apples

From the gold print, cut:
    6 piece #3 for center block apples
    6 piece #3 reversed for center block apples

    8 piece #9 for center border apples
    8 piece #9 reversed for center border apples
    8 piece #12 for corner border apples
    8 piece #12 reversed for corner border apples

From assorted red prints, cut:
    320 squares, each 2½" x 2½", or use
      Template #8 for multiple-squares border.

From the binding fabric, cut:
    1½"-wide bias strips to make 7 yds. of finished
      bias binding.

Directions

    Cut, piece, and appliqué the following, using the
templates on pages 32–33 and the pullout pattern
insert. Make plastic templates (page 84) for all
templates except the apples. Use freezer paper for
apple templates. Use ¼"-wide seam allowances for
all pieced seams.

Center Block

1. Appliqué the stem, then the leaves (piece #2).
   Next appliqué the apples. Using the freezer-
   paper method (page 84) for the apples, pin
   pieces #3 and #3 reversed in place, then
   appliqué pieces #4, #4 reversed, and #5.

2. Sew the red-print 1½"-wide inner border strips
   to the center block, mitering the corners. (See
   pages 88–89.)

Mitered inner border

Center Block Unit

Flying Geese Border

1. Piece 48 Flying Geese units. Press seams toward the large triangle. Sew together 12 Flying Geese units to make 4 Flying Geese strips.

Flying Geese Unit
Make 48

Flying Geese Strip
Make 4

2. Sew the Flying Geese strips to the inner border as shown.

Center Block Unit

2. Piece 6 rows of 20 red 2½" squares. Sew 3 rows together to make 2 top and bottom border units.

Top and Bottom Border Unit
Make 2

3. Sew the border units to the center block unit, adding the sides first, then the top and bottom.

Multiple-Squares Border

1. Piece 6 rows of 14 red print 2½" squares. Sew 3 rows together to make 2 side border units.

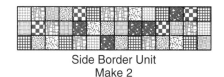

Side Border Unit
Make 2

Vine Border

1. Appliqué 46" of the vine bias in place on each 8½" x 56½" off-white border strip, leaving the 2 ends (1½") unstitched. Appliqué 18 leaves (piece #2) on each strip as indicated. Appliqué the center border apples; first pin pieces #9 and #9 reversed, then stitch #10, #10 reversed, and #11.

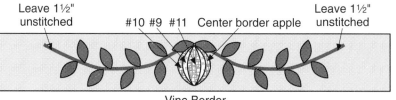

Leave 1½" unstitched   #10 #9 #11   Center border apple   Leave 1½" unstitched

Vine Border
Make 4
Finished size: 8½" x 56½"

2. Sew the vine borders to the multiple-squares borders, mitering the corners.

3. Complete the appliqué of the vines in the corners of the border. Appliqué the corner border apples in place, first pinning pieces #12 and #12 reversed, then stitching pieces #13, #13 reversed, and #14. Appliqué the remaining 8 leaves in the 4 corners.

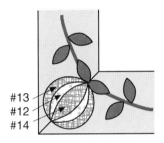

Single-Squares Border

1. Piece 2 rows of 28 red print 2½" squares to make 2 side border units.
2. Piece 2 rows of 30 red print 2½" squares to make 2 top and bottom border units.
3. Sew the border units to the center block unit.

Finishing the Quilt

Layer the quilt top with batting and backing. Quilt as desired and bind the edges. See "Quilt Finishing" on pages 89–93.

Audrey's Apple/Tea Cooler

"In our travels around the world we have had the opportunity to taste and test many delicious dishes and drinks. I don't remember where we first had this Apple/Tea Cooler, but it is served often in our home."

As an Air Force wife, Audrey Waite has visited and lived in many of the countries of the world. Retired and living in Sedona, Arizona, the Waites host the Quilted Apple Club Retreat each summer.

4 cups boiling water
4 herbal tea bags
4 cups apple juice
6 cinnamon sticks (optional)
6 orange slices (optional)

Steep teabags in boiling water for 5 minutes. Remove teabags and add apple juice. Stir well. Refrigerate until well chilled. Pour over ice cubes in 6 glasses. Add a cinnamon stick and an orange slice if desired. Serves 6.

◆

THE FRIENDLY COW ALL RED AND WHITE,
 I LOVE WITH ALL MY HEART:
SHE GIVES ME CREAM WITH ALL HER MIGHT,
 TO EAT WITH APPLE TART.

—Robert Louis Stevenson
A Child's Garden of Verses
"The Cow"

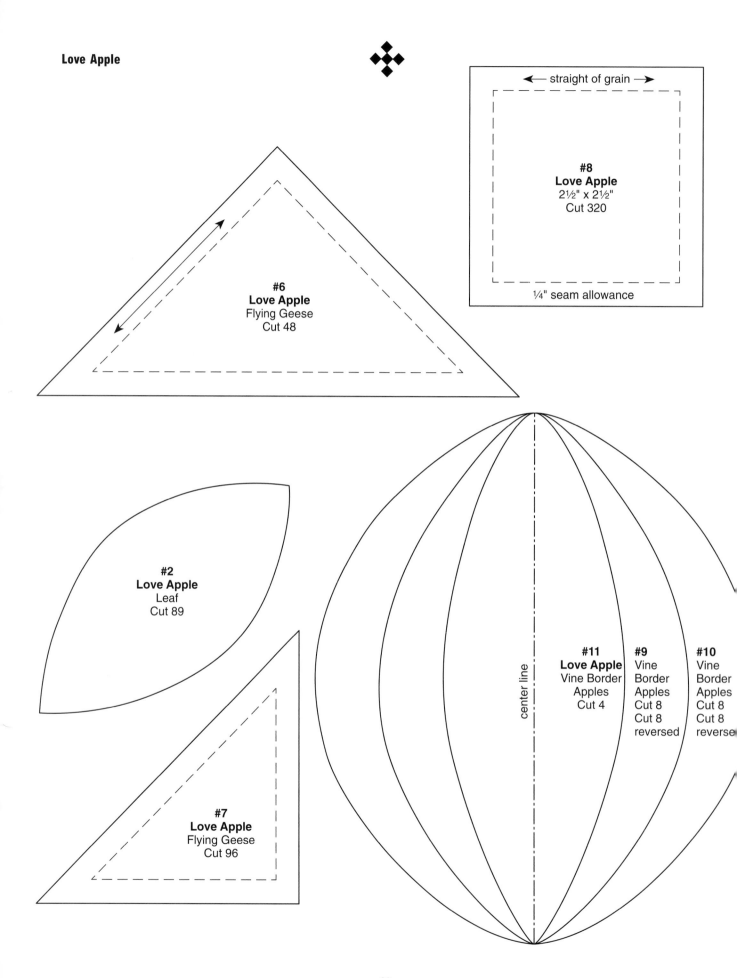

#6
Love Apple
Flying Geese
Cut 48

#8
Love Apple
2½" x 2½"
Cut 320

straight of grain

¼" seam allowance

#2
Love Apple
Leaf
Cut 89

#7
Love Apple
Flying Geese
Cut 96

center line

#11
Love Apple
Vine Border
Apples
Cut 4

#9
Vine
Border
Apples
Cut 8
Cut 8
reversed

#10
Vine
Border
Apples
Cut 8
Cut 8
reverse

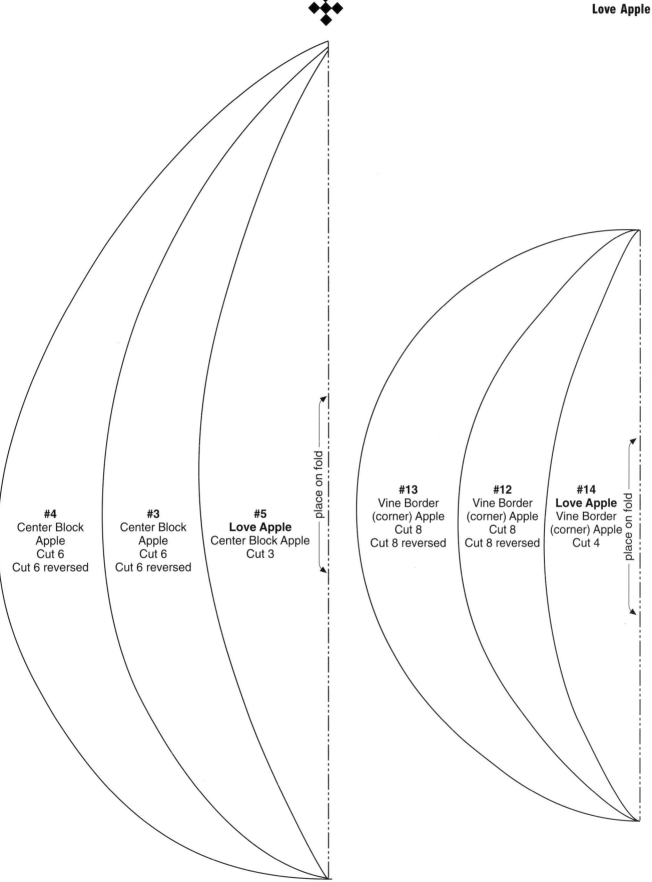

#4
Center Block
Apple
Cut 6
Cut 6 reversed

#3
Center Block
Apple
Cut 6
Cut 6 reversed

#5
Love Apple
Center Block Apple
Cut 3

place on fold

#13
Vine Border
(corner) Apple
Cut 8
Cut 8 reversed

#12
Vine Border
(corner) Apple
Cut 8
Cut 8 reversed

#14
Love Apple
Vine Border
(corner) Apple
Cut 4

place on fold

"A" is for Apple

Template #6
Corner Apple

Finished Quilt Size: 40" x 57"
Photo: page 45

Baby quilts are a "must" at The Quilted Apple. Many of our customers and students are expectant mothers or grandmothers who want to make a quilt for the newest addition to their families.

In the 1920s and 1930s when redwork embroidery was popular, some creative quiltmakers preferred blue. Hence, bluework was born.

The 1930 reproduction fabrics with all their pure colors keep the traditional look of "baby" pastels. However, a burst of brightness is added with the deep reds.

Our baby quilt combines bluework with appliqué and piecing using the Aunt Grace's reproduction fabrics. Claudia Dinnell machine pieced, appliquéd, and quilted this delightful baby quilt.

Materials
44"-wide fabric

3³/₄ yds. white for center panels, border triangles, inner and outer corner squares, and backing

1³/₄ yds. blue solid for corner triangles and binding

9" x 9" piece each of 6 different red prints for apples

9" x 16" piece each of blue, red, and yellow prints for cats

8" x 8" piece each of red, green, blue, and yellow prints for balls

6" x 6" piece of green solid for soccer ball

¹/₈ yd. each of 12 different prints for pieced border

3 yds. fusible web for machine appliqué

3 yds. tear-away stabilizer for machine appliqué

45" x 60" piece of batting

Blue permanent marking pen

3 skeins of blue (#312) DMC embroidery floss

Templates and lettering designs are on pages 38–44 and on the pullout pattern insert.

Cutting

For machine appliqué, do not add seam allowances to the appliqué pieces. For hand appliqué, add a scant ¹/₄"-wide seam allowance to each piece.

From the white, cut:
3 rectangles, each 15¹/₂" x 30¹/₂", for center panels
4 piece #17 for outer corner squares
204 piece #14 (or use preprinted grid paper to speed-piece inner border triangle units; see page 83)
4 piece #15 for inner border

From the blue solid, cut:
204 piece #14 (or use preprinted grid paper)

From 5 of the red print 9" squares, cut:
1 of pieces #1–#5, each from a different print

From the remaining red print 9" square, cut:
4 piece #6 (apple, stem, and leaf) for outer corner squares

From the 9" x 16" blue print, cut:
1 piece #7 (cat)

From the 9" x 16" red print, cut:
1 piece #8 (cat)

From the 9" x 16" yellow print, cut:
1 piece #9 (cat)

From the 8" x 8" red print, cut:
1 piece #10 (football)

From the 8" x 8" green print, cut:
1 piece #11 (soccer ball)

From the 8" x 8" blue print, cut:
1 piece #12 (basketball)

From the 8" x 8" yellow print, cut:
1 piece #13 (baseball)

From the green solid, cut:
the pieces indicated on Template #11

From the 12 different prints, cut:
80 piece #16

Directions

Use ¹/₄"-wide seam allowances for pieced seams.

1. Using a blue permanent marking pen, trace the lettering onto the three white panels. Refer to the Quilt Plan for placement.

2. With 2 strands of blue embroidery floss, embroider the lettering, using the outline stitch. See "Embroidery Stitches" on page 87. Repeat for all of the panels.

3. Using a machine satin stitch, appliqué the apples, balls, and cats onto the panels, referring to the photo on page 45 and the Quilt Plan on page 34. See "Machine Appliqué" on page 87.

   On panel A, appliqué 4 apples (Templates #1, #2, #4, #5), stems, and leaves. On panel B, appliqué 3 balls (Templates #10–#12). Satin stitch the details on the balls first, then appliqué around the outside edges of the balls.

For the soccer ball, appliqué the green solid pieces first, then do the satin stitching. Appliqué only the sitting cat (Template #9) onto Panel C. Press. The remaining apple (Template #5), 2 cats, and ball (Template #13) will be appliquéd after the border is added.

Panel A

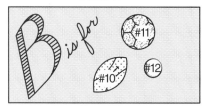

Panel B

Panel C

4. Appliqué 1 apple (Template #6), leaf, and stem to each of the 4 corner squares (Template #17). Press.

5. Stitch the blue and white triangles (Template #14) together to make 204 blue/white squares.

Make 160 blue/white squares.

6. Sew 29 blue/white squares together to make top and bottom inner-border strip units and panel divider strips. Press. Make 4.

29–Square Strip Unit
Make 4

7. Sew 44 blue/white squares together to make side inner-border strip units. Make 2. Stitch a white square (Template #15) to each end of each 44-square strip unit. Press.

44–Square Strip Unit
Make 2

8. For the top and bottom outer borders, piece together in random order 16 rectangles (Template #16). Make 2.

16 rectangles (Template #16)

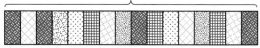

Top and Bottom Border Strips

9. For the side outer borders, piece together in random order 24 rectangles (Template #16). Make 2. Stitch an appliquéd apple corner square (made in step 4) to each end of each side outer-border strip. Press.

24 rectangles (Template #16)

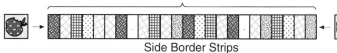

Side Border Strips

10. Stitch an inner-border strip unit to the top and bottom of panel A and to the bottom of panels B and C. Sew the panels together as shown.

36

11. Sew a side inner-border strip unit (made in step #7) to each side. Press.

12. Sew the top and bottom outer border strips (made in step #8) to the quilt top. Press.
13. Sew the side outer border strips (made in step #9) to the quilt top. Press.

14. Appliqué the remaining apple, ball, and cats onto the quilt top, referring to the photo and Quilt Plan for placement.

Finishing the Quilt

Layer the quilt top with batting and backing. Quilt as desired and bind the edges. See "Quilt Finishing" on pages 89–93.

APPLES—APPLES—APPLES
SAUCE AND CIDER AND CAKE AND PIE
TREAT FOR THE PALATE
FEAST FOR THE EYE

—Anonymous

"A" is for Apple

Satin stitch details.

#10
"A" is for Apple
Cut 1

#14
"A" is
for Apple

¼" seam allowance

#15
"A" is for Apple

straight of grain →

#16
"A" is for Apple
(2½" x 4½" cut)

#17
"A" is for Apple
(4½" x 4½" cut)

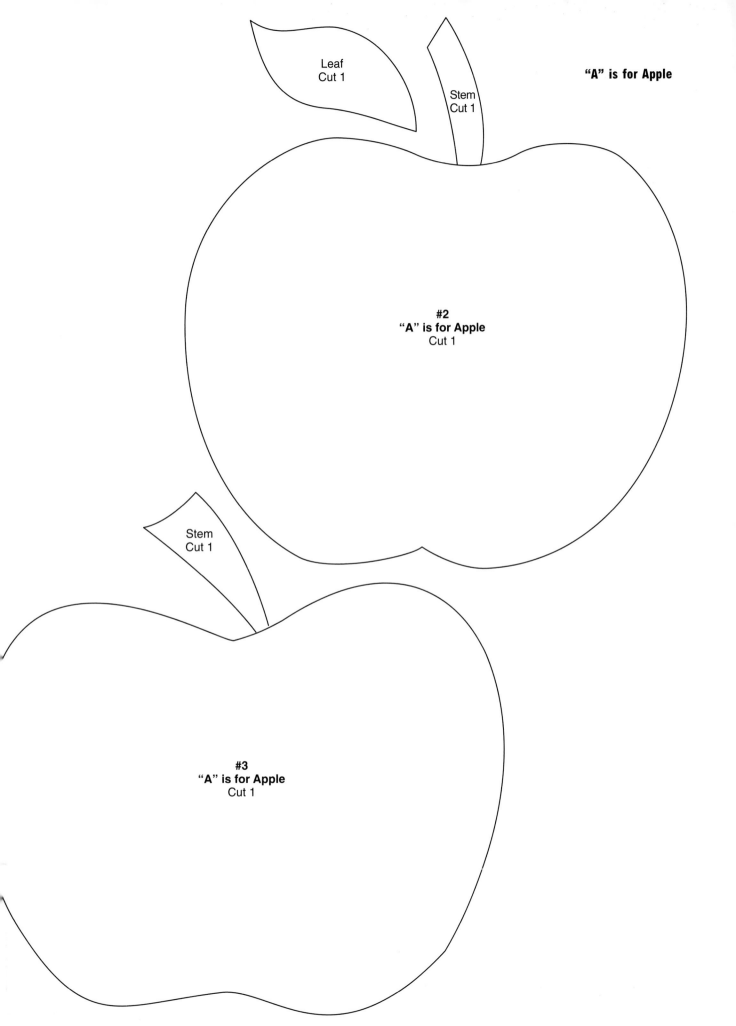

Leaf
Cut 1

Stem
Cut 1

"A" is for Apple

#2
"A" is for Apple
Cut 1

Stem
Cut 1

#3
"A" is for Apple
Cut 1

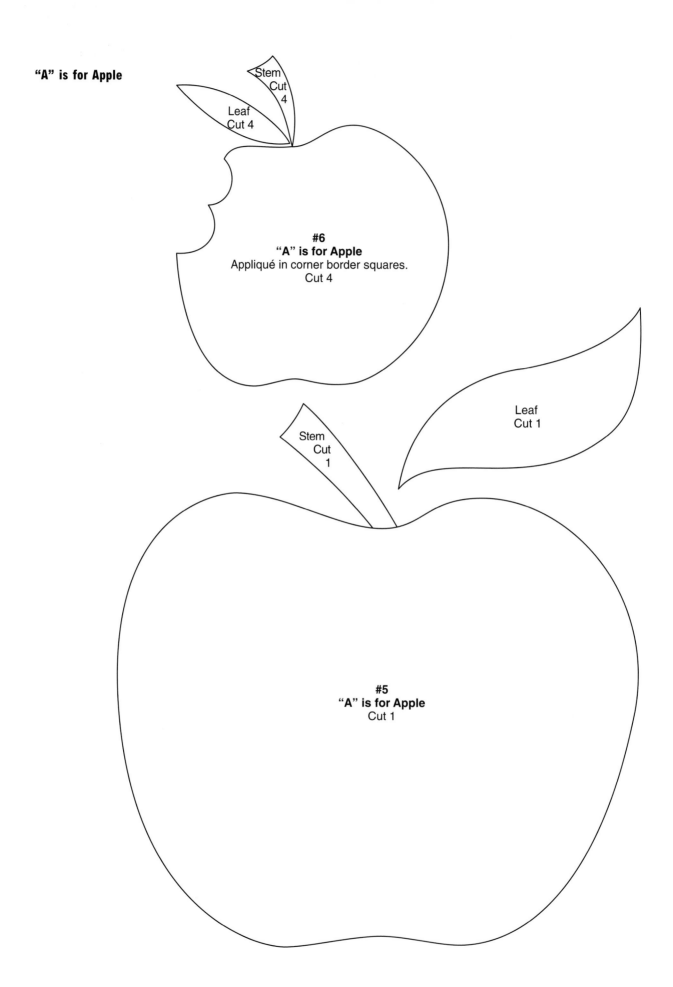

Stem
Cut
4

Leaf
Cut 4

#6
"A" is for Apple
Appliqué in corner border squares.
Cut 4

Leaf
Cut 1

Stem
Cut
1

#5
"A" is for Apple
Cut 1

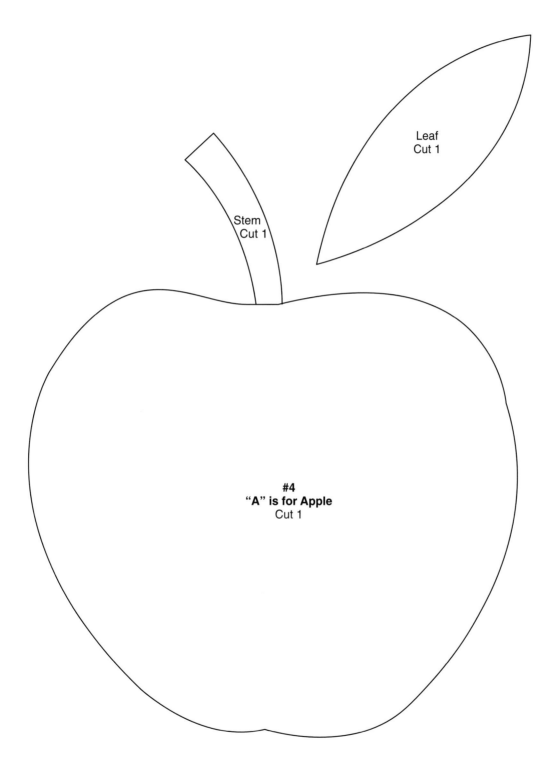

Leaf
Cut 1

Stem
Cut 1

#4
"A" is for Apple
Cut 1

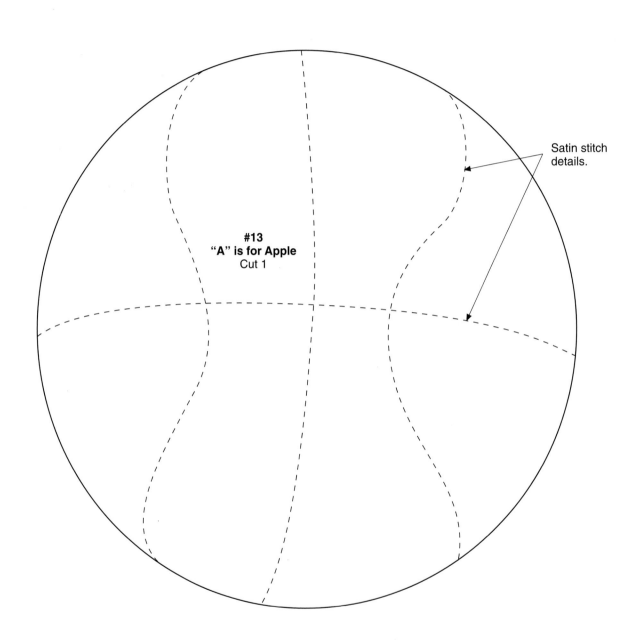

Satin stitch
details.

#13
"A" is for Apple
Cut 1

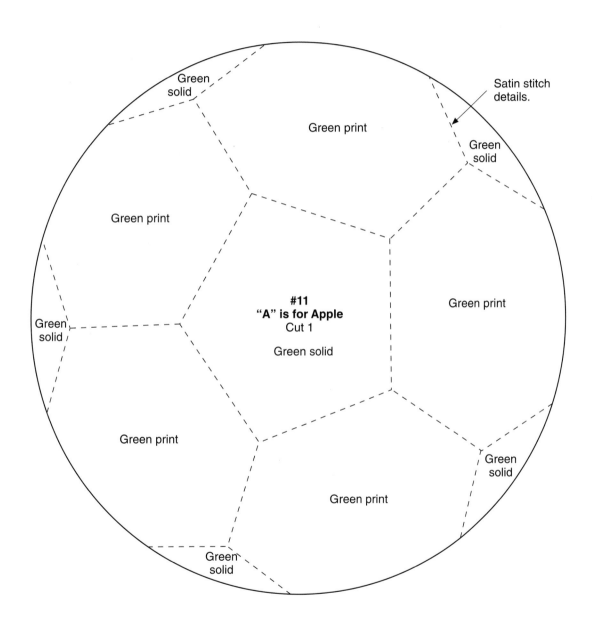

Green solid

Green print

Satin stitch details.

Green solid

Green print

Green print

Green solid

#11
"A" is for Apple
Cut 1

Green solid

Green print

Green print

Green solid

Green print

Green solid

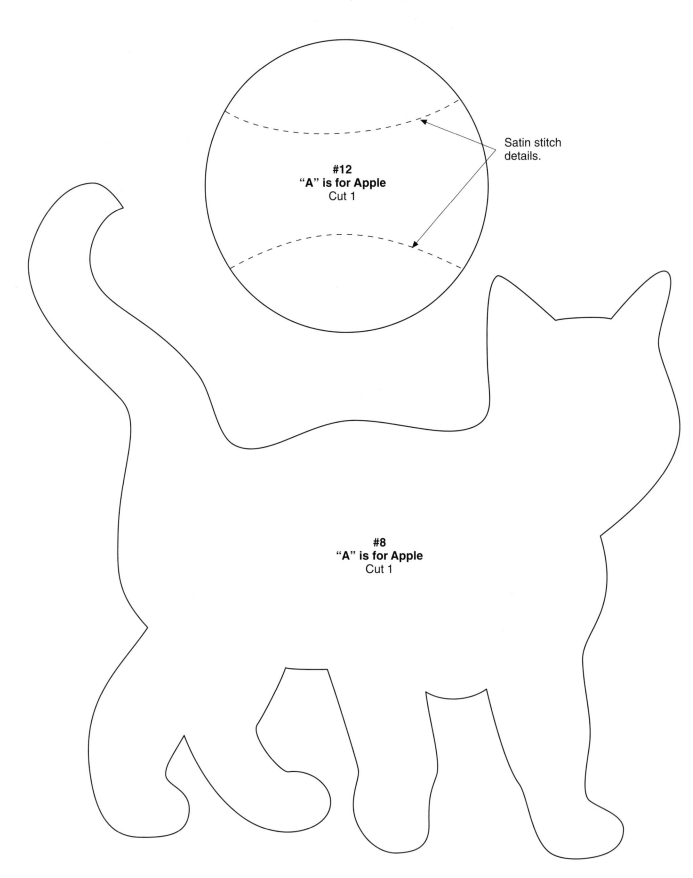

Satin stitch
details.

#12
"A" is for Apple
Cut 1

#8
"A" is for Apple
Cut 1

GALLERY OF QUILTS

"A" is for Apple, designed by Laurene Sinema, 1993, Phoenix, Arizona, 40" x 57". Bluework embroidery combined with the fresh 1930s "look-alike" fabrics make this baby quilt a delight. Machine appliquéd, pieced, and quilted by Claudia Dinnell, Phoenix, Arizona.

An Album Apple by Laurene Sinema, 1993, Phoenix, Arizona, 44" x 44".
This lovely quilt features a basket of apples surrounded by a vine of grapes and
apples that entwines under and over the pieced border. Quilted by Una Jarvis.

Apple Redwork Miniature (right), designed and set
together by Laurene Sinema, 1993, Phoenix,
Arizona, 15" x 15". Nine miniature blocks are
set together with a feather-stitched sashing
and border. These Friendship blocks were
embroidered by nine Quilted Apple Club members.

Log Cabin Apple (above), designed by Janet Carruth and Laurene Sinema, 1981, Phoenix, Arizona, 57½" x 85½". Polished apples add a new look to the center squares of a Log Cabin quilt. Quilted by Una Jarvis.

Apple Harvesttime Table Rug
by Laurene Sinema, 1993,
Phoenix, Arizona, 45" x 25".
This wool appliqué table rug
was inspired by nineteenth-
century "penny rugs."

Apple Days—School Days
by Laurene Sinema,
1993, Phoenix, Arizona,
40" x 60". Plaids and
checks combine to give
a primitive look to the
blocks and borders of
this charming quilt.
Quilted by Una Jarvis.

Love Apple by Laurene Sinema, 1993, Phoenix, Arizona, 60" x 60".
The love apple, a nineteenth-century design, is exciting today in this
combination of reds, greens, and golds. Quilted by Una Jarvis.

Left: A Hooked Apple (1993) by Janet Carruth, 1992, Phoenix, Arizona, 10½" x 10½". Red and green wool give the plump apple and its leaf a primitive look.

Center: A Redwork Apple (1994) by Laurene Sinema, 1993, Phoenix, Arizona, 12" x 12". The embroidered apple and grapes combined with the feather-stitched border are reminiscent of early twentieth-century redwork quilts.

Right: Our Logo Apple (1980), designed by Janet Carruth and Laurene Sinema, 1978, Phoenix, Arizona, 12" x 12". The Quilted Apple logo is as handsome in fabric as it is on paper. This 1993 version is pieced and appliquéd by Helen Ohlson.

Apple Pincushions, design adapted by Ginger Sanchez-Loupe, 1989, Phoenix, Arizona. Apples—big and small, red and green—make the perfect gift for a stitching friend.

Apple Picnic Quilt, designed by Janet Carruth and Laurene Sinema, 1993, Phoenix, Arizona, 51" x 51". Bright green and navy blue denim combine to make this happy quilt the perfect picnic cloth. Napkins and silverware fill the pockets of the tote, and the quilt folds to fit inside! Machine appliquéd, pieced, and quilted by Claudia Dinnell, Phoenix, Arizona.

Johnny Appleseed, designed by Laurene Sinema, 1993, Phoenix, Arizona, 25" x 35". This folk-art quilt celebrates the tale of a beloved folk hero, Johnny Appleseed. Appliquéd and pieced by The Quilted Apple staff and quilted by Lori Heikkila.

Johnny Appleseed

Finished Quilt Size: 25" x 35"
Photo: opposite page

A book of apple designs would not be complete without including Johnny Appleseed. For nearly two hundred years, tales of Johnny Appleseed have been told. Some of the stories are probably exaggerations or not true at all. However, Johnny Appleseed was a real person named John Chapman.

John was born in 1774 in Massachusetts. In 1795, he and Sarah Crawford were to be married.

Sarah became ill and died. What was to be their wedding day became her burial day. Sarah loved apple blossoms, and her beautiful apple blossom bridal bouquet was buried with her. As a memorial to his beloved Sarah, John vowed to cover the land with apple blossoms.

From that year until 1845, Johnny planted apple seeds in Ohio, Indiana, Illinois, and Pennsylvania. It is said that he carried only a bag of apple seeds, a walking stick, and a pan to cook in. Sometimes he wore the pan on his head because it was easier to carry that way. This tender Johnny Appleseed story is one to remember each time we see an apple tree in bloom!

My thanks to Quilted Apple staff members Barbara Voita, Lynda Brown, Helen Ohlson, Ann Bevilockway, Heidi Eberenz, Ginger Sanchez-Loupe, and Shirley Weagant for appliquéing this wall quilt. This little quilt is a great way to use some of those scraps or fat quarters that have been accumulating in your sewing room.

Materials
44"-wide fabric

1½ yds. total of assorted beiges for backgrounds and Hills-and-Valleys triangles

¼ yd. total of assorted greens for apple tree, pine tree, apple leaves, and Hills-and-Valleys triangles

⅛ yd. assorted reds for apples and Hills-and-Valleys triangles

⅛ yd. white-on-white print for apple blossoms

¼ yd. total assorted browns for tree trunk, walking stick, apple seeds, flagpole, and log cabin

Assorted scraps of red, blue, peach, red stripe, black, green, gold, brown, gray, beige, and tan for Johnny Appleseed, flag, apples, and stems

½ yd. dark green for inner border and binding

½ yd. tan plaid for outer border

1 yd. for backing

1 skein dark pink embroidery floss

1 skein light pink embroidery floss

1 skein black embroidery floss

Making the Blocks

Cut, piece, and appliqué the following blocks, using the templates on pages 58–61 and the pullout pattern insert. Make plastic templates, following the directions on page 84 for the apples and apple blossoms. Make freezer-paper templates (page 84) for the tree, Johnny Appleseed, flag, pine tree, bird, and log cabin. Appliqué the pieces in the numerical order indicated on the templates. Refer to the photo on page 52 and the Quilt Plan on page 53 for location of the pieces.

Apples Block

From assorted scraps for stems and leaves, cut:
5 each of pieces #1 and #2

From 5 assorted reds, greens, and golds, cut:
1 piece #3

From background fabric, cut:
1 rectangle, 3½" x 18½"

Appliqué pieces #1–#3 to the background.

Apples Block
Make 1
Finished size: 3" x 18"

Hills-and-Valleys Block

Hills and Valleys Block
Make 1
Finished size: 3" x 18"

From assorted beiges, cut:
6 piece #1
6 piece #3

From assorted greens, cut:
6 piece #2
3 piece #3

From assorted reds, cut:
6 piece #3

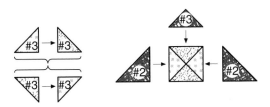

Hill Unit
Make 3
Finished size: 3" x 6"

Piece 3 Hill units to make 1 block.

Apple Blossoms Block

Apple Blossoms Block
Make 1
Finished size: 2" x 18"

From white-on-white print, cut:
9 pieces from Apple Blossom template
From background fabric, cut:
1 rectangle, 2$\frac{1}{2}$" x 18$\frac{1}{2}$"

Appliqué the blossom pieces to the background piece. Embroider the flower centers with a satin stitch, using 2 strands of dark pink embroidery floss. Embroider the petal details with an outline stitch, using 2 strands of light pink embroidery floss. See "Embroidery Stitches" on page 87.

Triple Rail Fence Block

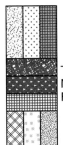

Triple Rail Fence Block
Make 1
Finished size: 3" x 9"

From 9 different fabrics, cut:
9 strips, each 3$\frac{1}{2}$" x 1$\frac{1}{2}$"

Cut and piece 3 Triple Rail Fence blocks, then sew them together.

Apple Tree Block

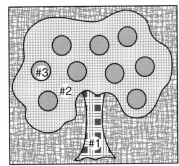

Apple Tree Block
Make 1
Finished size: 9" x 10"

From assorted browns, cut:
1 piece #1
From assorted greens, cut:
1 piece #2
From assorted reds, cut:
9 piece #3
From background fabric, cut:
1 rectangle, 10$\frac{1}{2}$" x 9$\frac{1}{2}$"

Appliqué pieces #1–#3 to the background.

Johnny Appleseed Block

Hat–Piece #11
Face–Piece #3
Arm–Piece #4
Walking Stick–Piece #5
Arm–Piece #6
Pants–Piece #7
Shirt– Piece #8
Vest–Piece #9
Bag–Piece #10
Foot–Piece #1
Foot–Piece #2

Johnny Appleseed Block
Make 1
Finished size: 5" x 9"

From scraps of peach, cut:
1 each of pieces #1–#4 and #6
From assorted scraps, cut:
1 each of pieces #5 and #7–#11
From background fabric, cut:
1 rectangle, 5$\frac{1}{2}$" x 9$\frac{1}{2}$"

Appliqué pieces #1–#11 to the background. Embroider the fingers, hair, jawline, and shirt-sleeve wrinkles with outline stitches, using 2 strands of black embroidery floss. See "Embroidery Stitches" on page 87.

Appleseeds Block

Appleseeds Block
Make 1
Finished size: 1" x 18"

From assorted browns, cut:
10 pieces from Apple Seed template
From background fabric, cut:
1 rectangle, 1½" x 18½"

Use reverse appliqué to appliqué appleseed pieces on the background piece. See "Reverse Appliqué Made Easy" on page 57.

Log Cabin Block

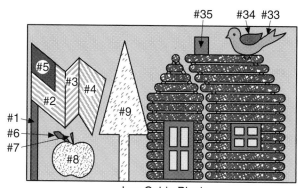

Log Cabin Block
Make 1
Finished size: 10" x 18"

From assorted scraps, cut:
1 each of pieces #1–#9, #11, #12, #13, #13r, #22, #23, and #25–#32
4 each of piece #10
2 each of pieces #14 and #21
6 each of pieces #15 and #16
3 each of pieces #24 and #17–#20
1 square, 1" x 1", for chimney (piece #35)
From background fabric, cut:
1 rectangle, 18½" x 10½"

Piece and appliqué 1 block. Use reverse appliqué for the window and door. See "Reverse Appliqué Made Easy" on page 57.

1. Appliqué piece #1 to the background. Refer to the color photo on page 52 for placement. Sew pieces #2, #3, and #4 together. Appliqué the resulting unit to the background. Appliqué piece #5 in place.

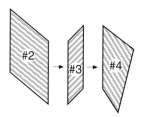

2. Appliqué pieces #6–#28 in place.
3. To give an illusion of depth between the glass panes and the wood frames of the door and window, appliqué these pieces using reverse appliqué. Pin pieces #29 and #31 in place. Use reverse appliqué for pieces #30 and #32.

Tip

Shirley made an overlay of the cabin on Mylar (you could use tracing paper instead) to use as a guide for placing the log cabin pieces. As she placed pieces, she lifted the Mylar guide, making it easier to put them in the proper location.

---

4. Appliqué pieces #33–#35 in place.
5. Embroider the bird legs and eye with an outline stitch, using 2 strands of black embroidery floss. See "Embroidery Stitches" on page 87.

Reverse Appliqué Made Easy

Reverse appliqué is a method that reveals an underneath fabric by cutting, turning under, and stitching the top layer of fabric. This method can be used with two or more layers.

1. Pin or baste two layers of fabric together. Draw the stitching line, then cut or slit only the top layer of fabric.
2. Turn the cut edges under to reveal the lower layer of fabric. Appliqué the top layer to the layer below it. Clip curves where necessary to get a smoothly turned edge.

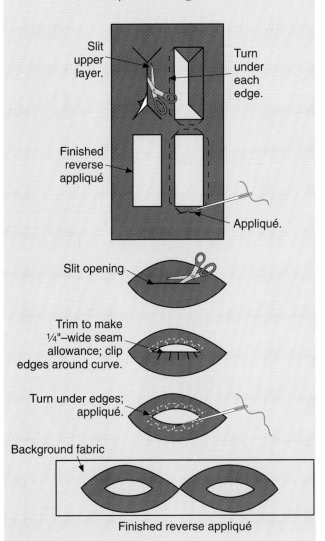

Assembling the Quilt Top

Use 1/4"-wide seam allowances.

1. Referring to the Quilt Plan on page 53 and the quilt photo on page 52, sew all the blocks together.
2. For the inner border, cut 2 strips, each 1" x 18 1/2", and 2 strips, each 1" x 29 1/2", from the dark green. Sew the 18 1/2"-long strips to the top and bottom of the quilt top. Sew the other 2 strips to the sides. Press seam allowances.
3. For the outer border, cut 2 strips, each 3 1/2" x 19 1/2", and 2 strips, each 3 1/2" x 35 1/2", from the tan plaid. Sew the 19 1/2"-long strips to the top and bottom, then sew the other 2 strips to the sides. Press seam allowances.

Finishing the Quilt

Layer the quilt top with batting and backing. Quilt as desired and bind the edges with straight-cut binding. See "Quilt Finishing" on pages 89–93.

REMEMBER JOHNNY APPLESEED,
    ALL YE WHO LOVE THE APPLE;
HE SERVED HIS KIND BY WORD AND DEED,
    IN GOD'S GRAND GREENWOOD CHAPEL.

—William Henry Venable
Johnny Appleseed

"Just after World War I, my grandmother and grandfather ran a boarding house in Besemer, Michigan. Apple Block was a favorite of the miners who boarded with them. My mother married and moved to Winslow, Arizona, where she worked at and contributed to every church fund-raiser, potluck dinner, and school and church bake sale. Apple Block became a favorite dessert at those events. It's homey and good, but fancy enough for company."

—Mary Dyer

Mary's Apple Block

2½ cups flour
1 teaspoon salt
1 cup lard*
1 egg
Milk
Cornflakes
8 cups apples, peeled and sliced
Sugar
Cinnamon
Margarine
1 egg white, slightly beaten

*Lard gives the crust in this dessert its distinctive flavor and texture.

Cut the lard into the flour and salt until coarse crumbs form. Beat the egg in a measuring cup and then add enough milk to make ⅔ cup. Add the egg/milk mixture to the flour/lard mixture to make a dough. Roll out a little more than half of the dough on a floured board until it is about ⅛" thick. Roll to fit a 9" x 13" pan. Place in pan so dough comes about 2" up the sides. Sprinkle a layer of cornflakes on bottom crust. Add apples, sprinkle generously with sugar and cinnamon, and dot with margarine. Roll remaining crust to fit pan; pierce with a fork. Place on top of apples and pinch edges of crust together. Brush top with slightly beaten egg white. Bake at 375°F for 1 hour or until nicely browned. Serves 8.

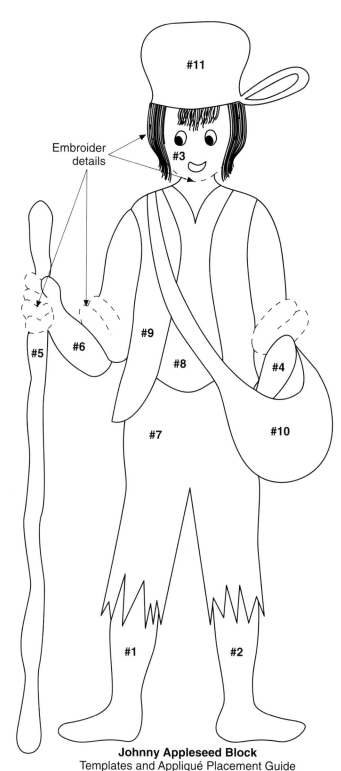

Johnny Appleseed Block
Templates and Appliqué Placement Guide

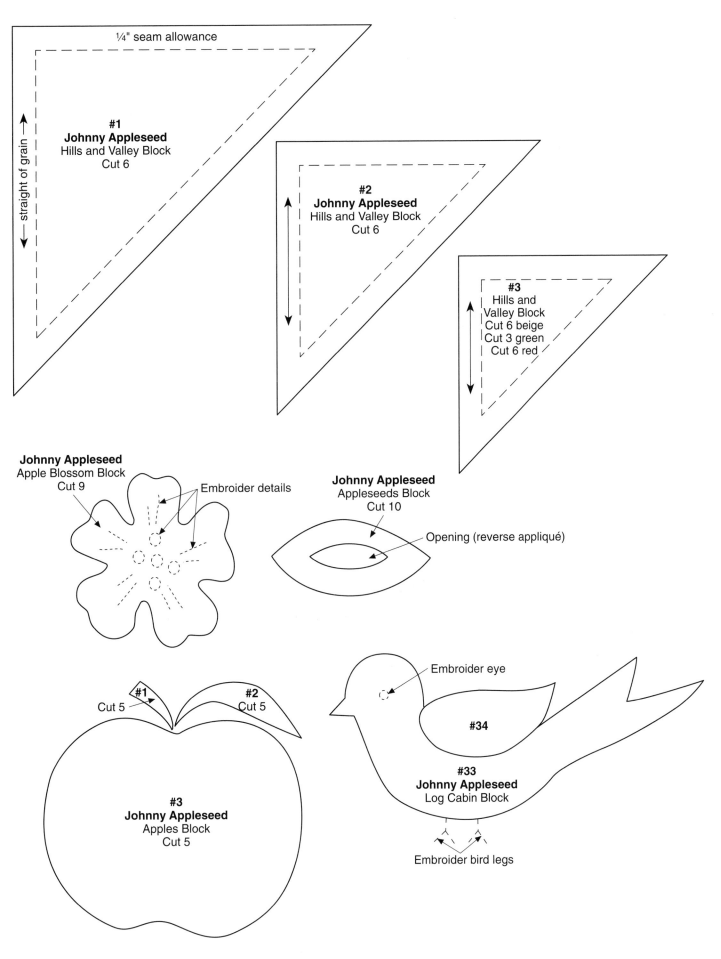

¼" seam allowance

#1
Johnny Appleseed
Hills and Valley Block
Cut 6

straight of grain

#2
Johnny Appleseed
Hills and Valley Block
Cut 6

#3
Hills and
Valley Block
Cut 6 beige
Cut 3 green
Cut 6 red

Johnny Appleseed
Apple Blossom Block
Cut 9

Embroider details

Johnny Appleseed
Appleseeds Block
Cut 10

Opening (reverse appliqué)

#1
Cut 5

#2
Cut 5

#3
Johnny Appleseed
Apples Block
Cut 5

Embroider eye

#34

#33
Johnny Appleseed
Log Cabin Block

Embroider bird legs

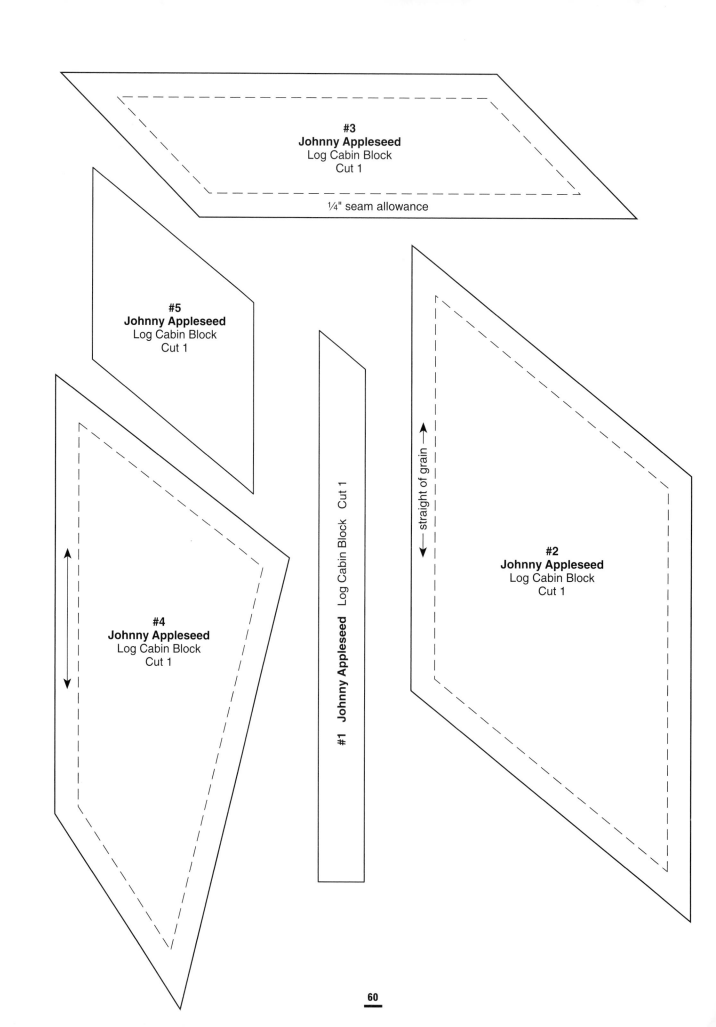

#3
Johnny Appleseed
Log Cabin Block
Cut 1

¼" seam allowance

#5
Johnny Appleseed
Log Cabin Block
Cut 1

straight of grain

#2
Johnny Appleseed
Log Cabin Block
Cut 1

#4
Johnny Appleseed
Log Cabin Block
Cut 1

#1   **Johnny Appleseed**   Log Cabin Block   Cut 1

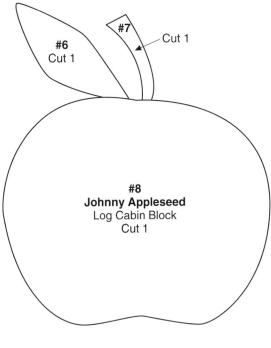

#6
Cut 1

#7
Cut 1

#8
Johnny Appleseed
Log Cabin Block
Cut 1

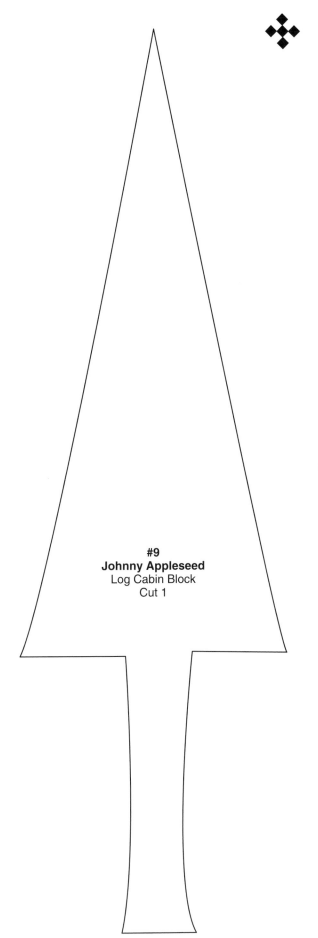

#9
Johnny Appleseed
Log Cabin Block
Cut 1

Log Cabin Apple

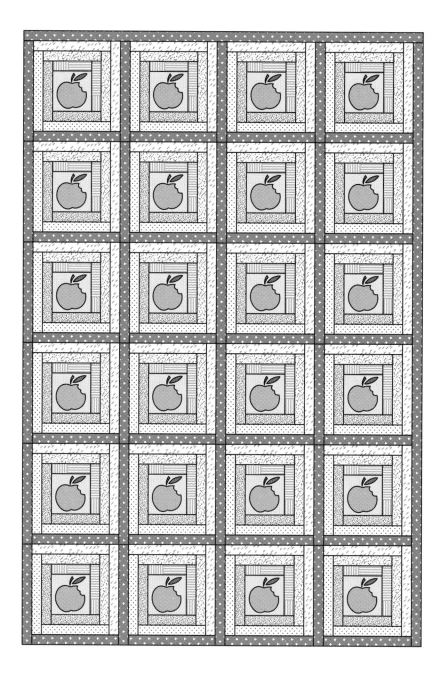

Finished Quilt Size: 57¹/₂" x 85¹/₂"
Photo: page 47

The Log Cabin design has long been a favorite of many quilters, both young and old. In 1981, Janet Carruth and I designed this Log Cabin quilt with a large center square. For added charm, we included apples in the centers of the log cabins. The dark and light corners add a three-dimensional effect.

Quilt down the center of each log—it gives the appearance of two narrower logs. A nifty trick!

Materials
44"-wide fabric

³/₄ yd. white for center squares
³/₄ yd. pink for apples
¹/₄ yd. green for stems and leaves
¹/₂ yd. Light #1 for logs
³/₄ yd. Light #2 for logs
1 yd. Light #3 for logs
³/₄ yd. Dark #1 for logs
1 yd. Dark #2 for logs
2 yds. Dark #3 for logs, borders, and binding
5 yds. fabric for backing
1 yd. fusible web for machine appliqué
1¹/₄ yd. tear-away stabilizer for machine appliqué

Cutting

For machine appliqué, do not add seam allowances to the appliqué pieces. For hand appliqué, add a scant ¹/₄"-wide seam allowance to each piece.

From the white, cut:
3 strips, each 5¹/₂" wide; crosscut into 21 squares, each 5¹/₂" x 5¹/₂". Cut 3 more squares, each 5¹/₂" x 5¹/₂", so you will have a total of 24 squares.

From the pink, cut:
24 piece #1 (apples)

From the green, cut:
24 piece #2 (leaves)
24 piece #3 (stems)

From Light #1, cut:
8 strips, each 2" x 42", for Logs A and B

From Light #2, cut:
12 strips, each 2" x 42", for Logs E and F

From Light #3, cut:
16 strips, each 2" x 42", for Logs I and J

From Dark #1, cut:
12 strips, each 2" x 42", for Logs C and D

From Dark #2, cut:
16 strips, each 2" x 42", for Logs G and H

From Dark #3, cut:
18 strips, each 2" x 42", for Logs K and L
10 strips, each 2" x 14¹/₂", for borders

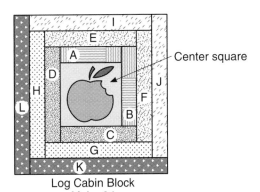

Log Cabin Block
Make 24
Finished size: 14" x 14"

Directions

Use ¹/₄"-wide seam allowances.

1. Using the template on page 65, appliqué by hand or machine an apple, stem, and leaf to each center square. See "Machine Appliqué" on page 87.

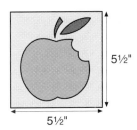

2. With right sides together, align the top edges of the appliquéd center squares on top of a Log A (Light #1) strip. Place them as close together as possible without overlapping them. Stitch. Continue until you have stitched all of the center squares to Log A. Cut between the squares. Press the seams toward the logs. Trim away excess fabric.

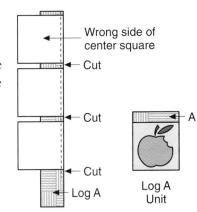

3. With Log A closest to you and with right sides together, place Log A units on top of a Log B (Light #1) strip. Place them as close together as possible without overlapping them. Stitch. Continue until you have stitched all of the Log A units to Log B. Cut between the squares. Press the seams away from the center. Trim away excess fabric.

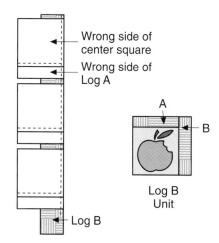

4. With Log B closest to you and with right sides together, place Log A/B units on top of a Log C (Dark #1) strip. Place them as close together as possible without overlapping them. Stitch. Continue until you have stitched all of the Log A/B units to Log C. Cut between the squares. Press the seams away from the center. Trim away excess fabric.

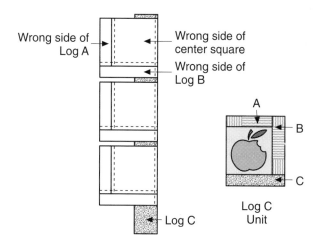

5. Continue adding logs in order as described above to complete 24 Log Cabin blocks.

6. Arrange the blocks with 4 blocks across and 6 blocks down. Sew the blocks together in horizontal rows; press the seams in opposite directions from row to row.

7. Match the seams between the blocks and sew the rows together.

8. Stitch 4 border strips (2" x 14½") together to make one length. With right sides together, pin the border to the top edge of the quilt top, matching the border seams with the seams between the blocks. Sew. Press the seam toward the border.

9. Stitch 6 border strips (2" x 14¼") together to make one length. Sew the border to the right side of the quilt top as described for the top border. Press the seam toward the border. The quilt top now has the Dark #3 fabric on all 4 sides.

Finishing the Quilt

Layer the quilt top with batting and backing. Quilt as desired. Bind the edges with 2"-wide bias strips cut from the Dark #3 fabric. See "Quilt Finishing" on pages 89–93.

Sandee's Applesauce Bread Pudding

"While visiting my sister on Orcas Island, Washington, we stayed at a charming bed and breakfast inn. The Turtleback Farm Inn served this delicious breakfast pudding. It is so good that we often serve it for dessert."

This testimony is from teacher, Sandee Streech. What do you think?

8 slices of raisin bread
$\frac{1}{2}$ cup butter, softened
1 cup applesauce, preferably homemade
$\frac{1}{2}$ cup white or brown sugar
2 teaspoons cinnamon
1 teaspoon nutmeg
$\frac{1}{2}$ cup raisins
3 cups milk
4 eggs
$1\frac{1}{2}$ teaspoons vanilla
Whipped cream

Spread butter on both sides of the raisin bread. Sauté on both sides until lightly toasted. Cut the slices into quarters. Place them in a 9" x 13" buttered baking dish. Spread applesauce over the top. Mix the sugar, cinnamon, and nutmeg together. Sprinkle the sugar mixture over the applesauce. Add the raisins. Blend the milk, eggs, and vanilla together and pour the mixture over the layers in the baking dish. Bake at 350° F for 30–35 minutes. The pudding should be puffed and golden brown. Serve warm with whipped cream. Serves 6.

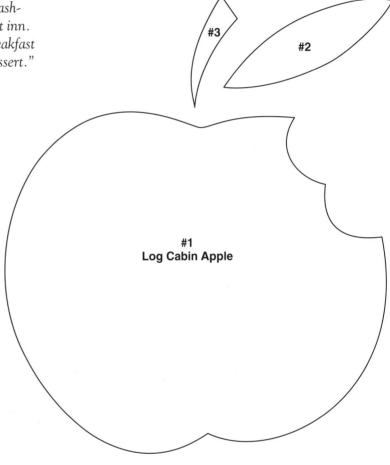

#3
#2
#1
Log Cabin Apple

◆

I TELL YOU, FOLKS, ALL POLITICS IS APPLESAUCE.

—Will Rogers
The Illiterate Digest

Apple Redwork Miniature

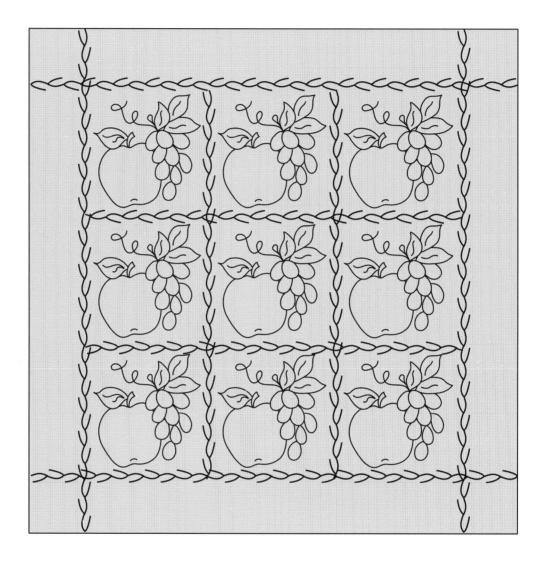

Finished Quilt Size: 15" x 15"
Photo: page 47

Each summer, The Quilted Apple Club has one meeting away from the heat of Phoenix. We have met in cool, beautiful Sedona the past two years. It is a weekend-long retreat with lots and lots of delicious food and hours and hours of stitching and talking. Last year, we discussed this book and the new designs for it. Cindy Taylor Oates suggested nine of the members each embroider an apple/grape redwork square. We decided to have a drawing for

the quilt after the book was completed. Linda Aiken, Gwen Albert, Val Benjamin, Janet Carruth, Claudia Dinnell, Mary Andra Holmes, Dee Lynn, Marian Sorci, and Audrey Waite all agreed. They embroidered and embroidered and finally a name was drawn—Gwen Albert was the lucky one!

You can make this a friendship block and have nine of your friends embroider one for you. Or you may wish to embroider all nine of them yourself. Either way, it is a dear little quilt.

Materials
44"-wide fabric

²/₃ yd. white or cream for background and backing
Red permanent marking pen
3 skeins of red (#498) DMC embroidery floss
16" x 16" piece of batting

Cutting

From the white or cream, cut:
    9 squares, each 4¹/₂" x 4¹/₂"
    1 square, 19" x 19", for the backing

Directions

Use ¹/₄"-wide seam allowances.
1. Center a 4¹/₂" fabric square over the apple/grape design on page 69. Use the red permanent marking pen to trace the design. Repeat with the remaining 4¹/₂" squares.
2. With 2 strands of red embroidery floss, embroider the design using the outline stitch. See "Embroidery Stitches" on page 87. Repeat for all the blocks.
3. Stitch the blocks together to make 3 rows, each having 3 blocks.

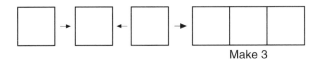

Make 3

4. Stitch rows together into a Ninepatch top.

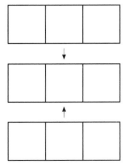

5. Layer the quilt top with the batting and backing, centering the quilt top. There will be a few inches of batting and backing around the outside edge of the quilt top. Pin or baste the layers together. Hand quilt in-the-ditch between the blocks.
6. With 2 strands of red embroidery floss, use the feather stitch to embroider over all the seams and the hand quilting. Do not stitch through to the backing!

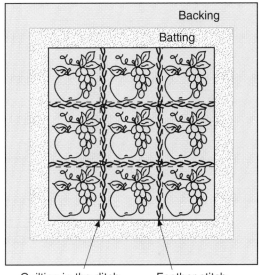

Quilting in-the-ditch   Feather stitch

7. Trim the batting to extend 1³/₄" outside the edge of the quilt top.

8. To create the borders, fold the backing up over the batting to the front as shown. Fold over the top and bottom edges first, then the sides. Turn under ¹/₄" seam allowances along the edges. Pin in place. Turn under ¹/₄"-wide seam allowances at the corners.

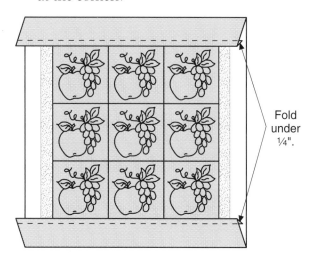

Fold under ¹/₄".

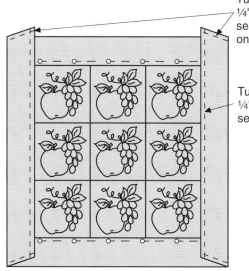

Turn under ¹/₄"-wide seam allowance on corners.

Turn under ¹/₄"-wide seam allowance.

9. Sew the borders in place by quilting in-the-ditch. Stitch the ends closed using a blind stitch.

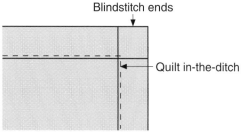

Blindstitch ends

Quilt in-the-ditch

10. Using 2 strands of red embroidery floss, embroider the feather stitch over the turned edges. Be sure to catch both the border and the quilt top as you stitch. Do not stitch through to the backing. Feather-stitch the corners as shown.

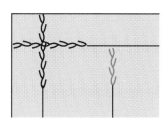

Marie's Apple Butter Sausages

Many years ago, my friend Marie Heaton served these yummy sausages at a brunch. They were a hit that day and continue to cause a sensation whenever I serve them. It's hard to believe that they are so easy!

2 cups apple butter
12 smoky sausages (Oscar Meyer)

In a saucepan, heat apple butter thoroughly. Add sausages and simmer until the sausages are heated through. Serves 4.

WHERE THE APPLE REDDENS
NEVER PRY—
LEST WE LOSE OUR EDENS,
EVE AND I.

—Robert Browning
A Woman's Last Word

Apple Redwork Miniature
Embroidery Design

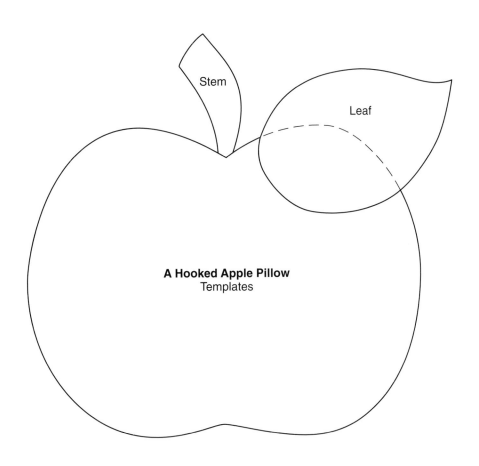

A Hooked Apple Pillow
Templates

Apple Pillows—A Birthday Treat

Each September, customers, students, friends, and staff enjoy a three-day long celebration to commemorate The Quilted Apple's birthday.

For our first birthday party, our friend Arlene baked tiny apple muffins and served them with cold apple juice to all who attended. Arlene spent the entire day baking and delivering apple muffins! The attendance was overwhelming and everyone enjoyed the muffins.

The following year we started a new annual tradition by arranging with a neighborhood bakery to make and deliver applesauce cookies. For four-teen years, the bakery has used the same recipe for our special occasion. Each year, we are asked for the secret recipe and unfortunately, it is not ours to share! However, we have Arlene's muffin recipe.

Exhibits of student quilts, demonstrations of new techniques or quilting notions, and a 25%-off sale of all shop merchandise are included in the festivities. Each year, we design an original Apple block pattern specifically for The Quilted Apple's birthday. Three of the designs are included here—Our Logo Apple (1980), A Hooked Apple (1993), and A Redwork Apple (1994).

◆

Our Logo Apple (1980)

Finished Size: 12" x 12"
Photo: page 50

Helen Ohlson, a member of our staff, stitched this pillow. She says the block is quick and easy. Enjoy!

Materials
44"-wide fabric

1/4 yd. dark print for patches and bias cording
1/4 yd. light print for patches
12½" x 12½" square of ecru and white print for pillow top
12½" x 12½" square of fabric for pillow back
Green print scrap for stem
54" long piece of 1/4" cording
12" x 12" pillow form

Cutting

Use templates on page 74.

From dark print, cut:
  6 piece A
  1 piece C
  54" of 1½"-wide bias strips to cover the cording

From light print, cut:
  4 piece A
  2 piece B
  2 piece D

From green scrap, cut:
  1 piece E

Directions

1. Assemble the rows as shown.

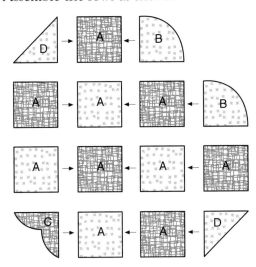

4. Center the pieced apple on the background square as shown in the Block Plan, leaving space at the top for the stem. Begin appliquéing at the top of the apple, to the left side of the stem and continue stitching around the apple. Stop stitching just to the right of the stem location. Appliqué the stem in place, then complete the apple appliqué. See "Appliqué Techniques" on pages 84–87.

5. Press. See "Pressing" on page 88.

6. Finish pillow with corded edge. See "Pillow Finishing" on pages 93–94.

Arlene's Spiced Apple Muffins

3 cups flour
4 teaspoons baking powder
2 teaspoons salt
1/2 cup shortening
2 eggs, well beaten
1 1/4 cups milk
1 cup grated apple

Preheat oven to 375°F. Combine first 3 dry ingredients. Cut in shortening. In a separate bowl, mix eggs and milk together; add flour mixture. Fold in apples. Spoon batter into well-greased, small (2" diameter around the top) muffin pans. Sprinkle with topping. Bake for 25 minutes. Makes 24 muffins.

Topping:
2 tablespoons sugar
1/4 teaspoon cinnamon

Mix sugar and cinnamon together.

2. Assemble the block as shown.

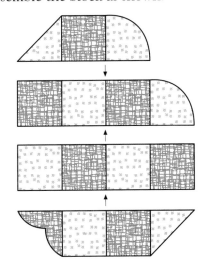

3. "Round out" the edges of the apple.

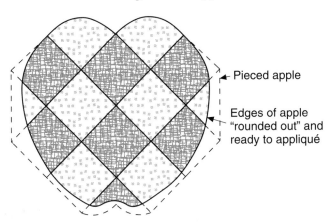

← Pieced apple

Edges of apple "rounded out" and ready to appliqué

A Hooked Apple (1993)

Finished Size: 10¹/₂" x 10¹/₂"
Photo: page 50

Janet Carruth has been making hooked rugs for years. Under her watchful eye, we established a rug-hooking corner and now have an extensive inventory of wool, burlap, and other supplies. In addition to teaching at The Quilted Apple, Janet has designed several beautiful rugs for us.

She designed this wonderful hooked apple. All you need are a few scraps of wool fabric, burlap, and a hook. Practice on a scrap of burlap first. After you have made this pillow, use it as inspiration to make a bushel-basket-of-apples rug!

Materials

Medium-weight, tightly woven wool fabrics:
   4" x 18" piece of red for the apple
   2" x 18" piece of green for the leaf
   ¹/₄" x 18" strip of brown for the stem
44"-wide cotton fabrics:
   ¹/₄ yd. green print for border
   ³/₄ yd. red print for back and ruffle
12" x 12" square of burlap for pillow top
Black fine-point permanent marking pen
Polyester fiberfill
Embroidery hoop (8" wooden)
Rug hook (medium)
   (See illustration at right.)

Cutting

From the wool, cut:
   ¹/₄"-wide strips*

From the green print, cut:
   2 strips, each 2¹/₂" x 7¹/₂", for border
   2 strips, each 2¹/₂" x 11", for border

From the red print, cut:
   2 strips, each 7" x 44", for ruffle
   1 square, 11¹/₂" x 11¹/₂", for pillow back

*Use a rotary cutter or a rug-wool cutting machine if you have one.

Directions

Use templates on page 69.
1. To eliminate raveling, apply masking tape or zigzag stitch around the outer edge of the burlap.
2. Make plastic templates of the apple, stem, and leaf. See "Templates for Appliqué" on page 84.
3. Center the templates on the burlap and draw around each with a black fine-point permanent marking pen.
4. Stretch the marked burlap in the embroidery hoop. Rest the hoop comfortably on a table or your knee.
5. Start with the outline of the apple design. Hold the hook in your right hand above the burlap backing and a strip of red wool in your left hand underneath the backing. (Reverse if you are left-handed.) To begin, push the hook through a mesh hole and pull the end of a wool strip through the burlap to the top, to a length of about ¹/₂". This "tail" will be trimmed flush with the loops later.
6. Insert the hook through the next hole and pull the first loop up to the top, making a ¹/₄" high loop. Continue pulling ¹/₄" loops to the top, until about ¹/₂" of the strip remains, then pull the tail to the top. Keep the loops even and consistent. Start a new strip in the same hole as the previous strip.

7. Fill in the design, working in any direction that seems easy for you. However, do not skip rows of the burlap mesh. Periodically, trim the tails flush with the pile, using small scissors.

Cut ends even with top of loops.

8. Continue in the same manner with leaf and stem.

9. Trim burlap square to 8" x 8". Add border strips, using ½"-wide seam allowances. See "Straight-Cut Borders" on page 88.

10. Finish pillow with ruffled edge. See "Ruffled-Edge Pillow" on page 94.

A Redwork Apple (1994)

Finished Size: 12" x 12"
Photo: page 50

This design, inspired by a redwork quilt of the 1920s, certainly fits into this book of apples. It was my desire to have a wide variety of apple designs and quilting techniques—so many that each of you would find the one apple project perfect for you. Perhaps this little pillow is the one.

Materials
44"-wide fabric

½ yd. white for pillow top and back
2 skeins DMC #498 red embroidery floss
12" x 12" square pillow form
Red permanent marking pen

Cutting

From white, cut:
1 square, 12½" x 12½", for pillow top
1 square, 12½" x 12½", for pillow back

Directions

Use pattern on page 75.

1. Center the pillow-top square on top of the apple/grape design. Hold the fabric taut (but not stretched) and trace the design onto the right side of the fabric, using a red permanent pen. Test your marker on a scrap of fabric first to make sure it doesn't bleed or that the line does not spread as you draw.

2. Use the outline stitch to embroider the design with 2 strands of red embroidery floss. See "Embroidery Stitches" on page 87.

3. Draw lines with a permanent pen 1¾" from the outside edges of pillow top.

4. Use the feather stitch to embroider the lines with 2 strands of red floss. See "Embroidery Stitches" on page 87.

5. Press pillow top and finish pillow with knife edges. See "Pressing" on page 88 and "Pillow Finishing" on page 93.

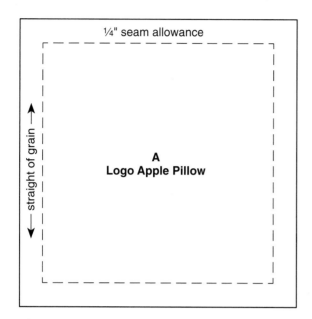

¼" seam allowance

straight of grain

A
Logo Apple Pillow

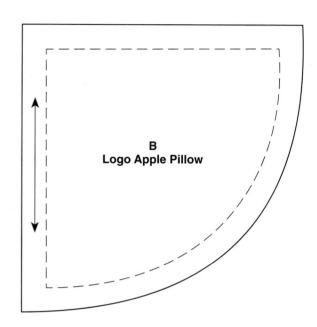

B
Logo Apple Pillow

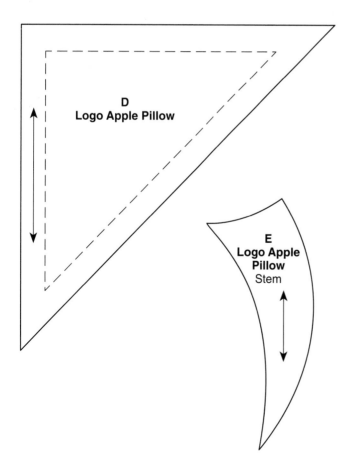

D
Logo Apple Pillow

E
Logo Apple Pillow
Stem

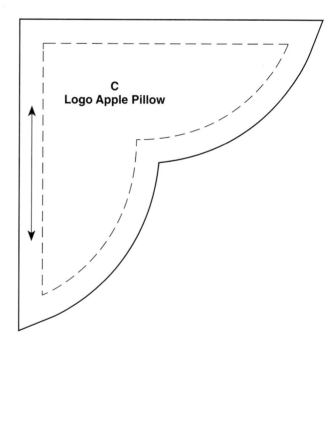

C
Logo Apple Pillow

A Redwork Apple Pillow
Embroidery Design

Apple Picnic Quilt and Tote Bag

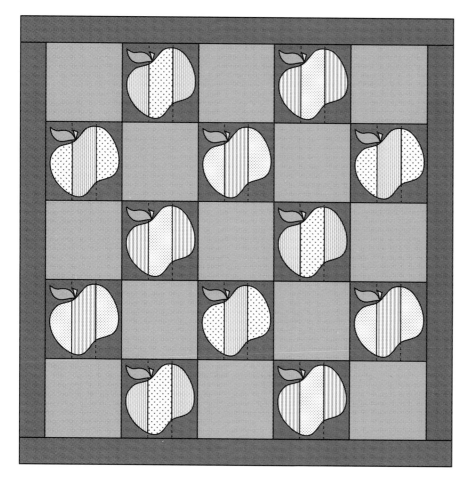

Finished Quilt Size: 51" x 51"
Photo: page 51

Finished Tote Bag: 14" x 14"
Photo: page 51

Fried chicken, potato salad, watermelon, brownies, and Audrey's Apple/Tea Cooler (page 31)—all this under a tree, near a stream on a lovely, warm day. It makes you want to plan a picnic, doesn't it? So, you'll need the Apple Picnic Quilt and Tote Bag. Not only will you have a grand time stitching them, but you will be so organized for your next picnic!

The picnic quilt folds up and fits inside the tote, which also has pockets for napkins and silverware. We love denim teamed with this shade of green. We lined the tote and backed the quilt with an apple print. These are quick to make because they are machine pieced, appliquéd, and quilted.

Materials
44"-wide fabric

¹/₃ yd. each of 2 different reds for apples
¹/₃ yd. each of 2 different blues for apples
2 yds. green for leaves, alternate blocks, and
    napkins
2" x 18" scrap of brown for stems
2 yds. 60"-wide denim for background blocks,
    border, binding, and tote bag
3¹/₄ yds. apple print for quilt backing and tote-bag
    lining
2 yds. fusible web
2 yds. tear-away stabilizer for machine appliqué
56" x 56" piece of batting for quilt
5¹/₂" x 43" piece of batting for tote bag
2 squares of batting, each 14¹/₂" x 14¹/₂", for tote
    bag

Directions

Cut, piece, and appliqué the following blocks, using the template on the pullout pattern insert. Use ¹/₄"-wide seam allowances.

Apple Blocks

1. From each of the 2 red and 2 blue fabrics, cut 3 strips, each 3¹/₂" x 42".
2. Sew 3 strips of red fabric together and 3 strips of blue together. Make 2 sets of red and 2 sets of blue. Press seams. (See page 88.)

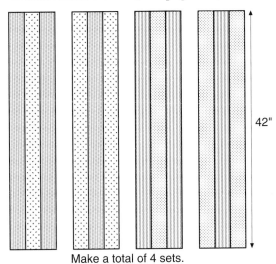

42"

Make a total of 4 sets.

3. Make plastic templates of the apple, stem, and leaf. Mark the seam lines on the apple template and mark the top of the apple with an X. Mark the right side on the stem and leaf templates.
4. With the right side of the template facing up, trace around the apple template onto the paper side of 9" squares of fusible web. Mark the apple seam lines. Make 14.

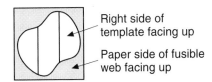

Right side of
template facing up

Paper side of fusible
web facing up

5. Align the traced seam lines on the fusible-web apples with the seam lines of the 3-strip units. Iron the fusible web onto the wrong side of the 3-strip units. Cut the apples out of the fabric, using the traced lines as guides.
6. With the right sides of the templates facing up, trace around the stem and leaf templates onto the paper side of the fusible web. Make 14 of each.
7. Iron the fusible web leaves onto the wrong side of the green fabric and the fusible-web stems onto the wrong side of the brown fabric. Cut out the stems and leaves on the traced lines.
8. From denim, cut 14 squares, each 9¹/₂" x 9¹/₂".
9. Remove the paper from the fusible web and position the apples, stems, and leaves on the denim squares. Iron them in place.

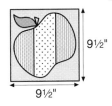

9½"

9½"

10. Machine appliqué the apples, stems, and leaves on 12 blocks. Set 2 blocks aside for the tote bag. See "Machine Appliqué" on page 87.

Picnic Quilt

1. From the green fabric, cut 13 squares, each 9¹/₂" x 9¹/₂".
2. Sew Apple blocks alternately with green blocks in rows of 5 blocks each, using ¹/₄"-wide seam allowances. Make 5 rows. Sew the rows together. Refer to the Quilt Plan on page 76.

3. From the denim, cut 2 strips, each 3½" x 45½", for the side borders, and 2 strips, each 3½" x 51½", for the top and bottom borders.

4. Sew the side borders to the quilt top, then add the top and bottom borders.

5. From the apple print, cut 2 strips, each 28" x 56". With right sides together, sew the 2 strips together. Press seams.

6. Layer the quilt top with the batting and backing; baste.

7. Machine quilt, using the seam lines in the pieced apples and the seam lines between the blocks to establish the vertical quilting lines. For the horizontal quilting lines, quilt in-the-ditch between the rows. Bind the edges with straight-cut binding cut from the denim. See "Binding" on pages 91–93.

Tote Bag

Use ¼"-wide seam allowances.

1. Satin-stitch the top edge only of the 2 remaining Apple blocks.

2. From the denim, cut 2 squares, each 14½" x 14½", for the front and back panels and 1 strip, 5½" x 43", for the boxing strip.

3. Center an apple block on the front panel. Satin stitch in place, leaving the top edge unstitched to form a pocket. Repeat for the back panel.

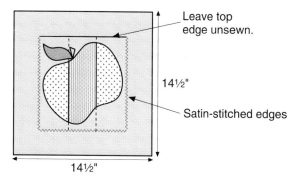

Leave top edge unsewn.

14½"

14½"

Satin-stitched edges

4. From the apple print, cut 1 strip, 5½" x 43", for the boxing-strip lining, and 2 squares, each 14½" x 14½", for the front and back panel linings.

5. Place the 5½" x 43" batting strip on the wrong side of the boxing-strip lining fabric. Sew them together along the long sides, using a zigzag stitch.

6. Place a 14½" square of batting on the wrong

side of each 14½" x 14½" lining square. Zigzag around all sides.

7. Mark the centers of the linings for the front and back panels by folding them in half. Notch at the fold line. Fold the boxing strip in half crosswise and notch at the fold line.

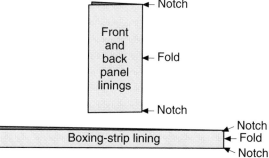

Notch

Front and back panel linings

Fold

Notch

Boxing-strip lining

Notch
Fold
Notch

8. Pin boxing-strip lining to front panel lining, right sides together, aligning the edges and matching the notches. Clip ¼" into the seam allowance of the bottom corners of the boxing strip. Stitch the 2 pieces together. Stitch back-panel lining to the boxing-strip lining in the same manner.

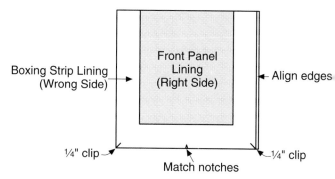

Boxing Strip Lining (Wrong Side)

Front Panel Lining (Right Side)

Align edges

¼" clip

¼" clip

Match notches

9. With the denim front panel, back panel, and boxing strip, repeat step 8 above. You now have a denim bag and a lining bag.

10. From the denim, cut 2 strips, each 6" x 14", for the handles.

11. Fold the handle strips in half lengthwise with wrong sides together. Press. Open out and refold with raw edges meeting in the middle at the pressed fold line. Press. Fold in half again so that you have a 1¼" x 14" finished strip. Topstitch ¼" from the edge on both sides of the handles. Topstitch again down the middle of the handle.

¼"

¼"

12. Turn the denim bag right side out and the lining bag wrong side out. Place the lining bag inside the denim bag, matching the seam lines and top edges. Pin.

13. Position 1 handle as shown on the denim bag. Stitch in place. Repeat on other side of the bag.

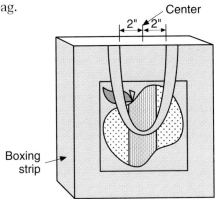

14. From the denim, cut 1 strip, 2½" x 38½", for the binding. Stitch the ends together. With wrong sides together, fold it in half lengthwise. Press. Pin the binding to the outside of the bag, aligning the raw edges. Stitch. Turn the binding strip to the inside and hand stitch in place.

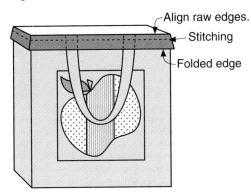

15. Using the seam lines in the apples to establish the stitching line, stitch through all the layers as shown to form 3 pockets. Repeat on the other side of the bag.

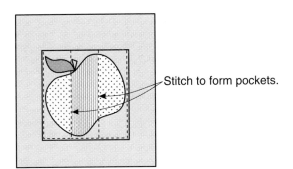

Napkins

From green fabric, cut 4 squares, each 15" x 15". Hem the edges by turning under ¼" twice; stitch, using a zigzag or straight stitch. (A serger may be used instead.)

NOT EVERYONE HAS THE SAME TASTE, BUT THERE'S AN APPLE FOR EVERY TASTE.

—Anonymous

Apple Pincushions

Photo: page 50
The Quilted Apple had only been open a few months when a very engaging young mother brought in a small bushel basket of these dear apple pincushions. She asked if we would be interested in selling them in our shop. We ordered several dozen and waited for delivery. Finally, several apples arrived. We were disappointed to have received only a few. We ordered more and again only a few arrived. We told her that we would take all the apples she could make. "Even a hundred?" she asked. "Yes!" we answered. Again we waited patiently, and again only a few apples were delivered. Our customers loved them and we knew that we could sell many more.

Eventually, our "apple maker" moved away. Ginger Sanchez-Loupe, who has been working at The Quilted Apple for several years, adapted the pattern and became our in-house "apple maker." When it is time to make apples, Ginger and her four daughters form an assembly line and make a hundred or more at one time. The Quilted Apple sells "an apple a day" throughout the year. We are happy to share the pattern with you.

Materials
44"-wide fabric

For a small apple pincushion:
  6" x 6" piece of red or green for apple
  4" x 6" piece of green for leaf
  4" length of ³/₈"-wide green double-faced satin ribbon

For a large apple pincushion:
  8" x 8" piece of red or green for apple
  4" x 8" piece of green for leaf
  4¹/₂" length of ³/₈"-wide green double-faced satin ribbon

Polyester fiberfill
Off-white Knit-Cro-Sheen thread

Fusible web
Tear-away stabilizer
5"-long doll needle
Hot-glue gun and glue

Directions

1. Make plastic templates, following the directions on page 84. Use the templates on pages 81–82. The templates include ¹/₄"-wide seam allowances.
2. Fold the red or green fabric square in half with right sides together. Align the template on the fold line as indicated. Trace around the template, then cut the apple out on the traced line.

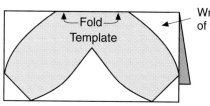

3. Fold the apple as shown with right sides together. Machine stitch ¹/₄" inside the traced lines.

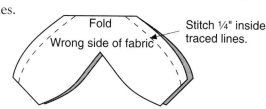

4. Refold the apple and stitch ¹/₄" inside the remaining 2 traced lines.

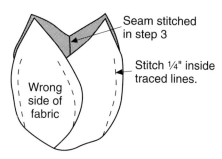

5. Turn the apple right side out. Make a gathering thread around the top of the apple by laying an 18" length of Cro-Sheen thread ¼" from the raw edge and zigzag stitch over the Cro-Sheen as shown.

Wrong side of fabric

Zigzag over Cro-Sheen thread.

6. Stuff the apple with the fiberfill until it is firm.

7. Cut the piece of green leaf fabric in half lengthwise. Use fusible web to bond the 2 pieces with wrong sides together. Place the leaf pattern on the bonded fabric, draw around it, and cut the leaf out on the traced line.

8. Place the leaf on top of a piece of stabilizer that has been cut to a size slightly larger than the leaf. Satin-stitch around outside edge of the leaf. Tear away the stabilizer.

9. Thread a 5"-long doll needle with a 24" length of Cro-Sheen thread. Tie a knot at one end of the thread.

10. Insert the needle through the center of the leaf and bring it through the bottom of the apple, leaving the knot on top. Take a ¼"-long stitch and return it to the top of the apple. Pull the thread snugly to form a dimple on the bottom of the apple. Make another stitch through the center of the leaf. Make a knot next to the first knot.

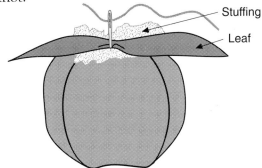

Stuffing

Leaf

11. To make the stem, fold the ribbon in half to form a loop. Glue the ends together. Glue the stem to the center of the leaf, covering the Cro-Sheen knots.

12. Pull the ends of the gathering thread a little more, then add more fiberfill. Repeat until the apple is firm. As you gather the fabric, the top

raw edges are pulled down into the apple, and the leaf and stem stands up. Gather securely and tie under the leaf.

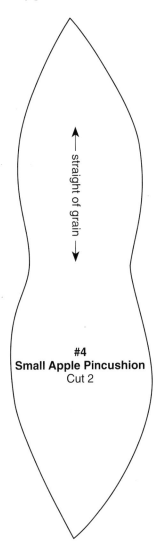

Creative Option: *Make a batch of these apples for holiday decorations—ornaments on your tree or a basketful for a festive dining-table centerpiece. Use elegant velvets, silks, and brocades or some of the wonderful holiday printed cottons!*

straight of grain

#4
Small Apple Pincushion
Cut 2

Apple Pincushions

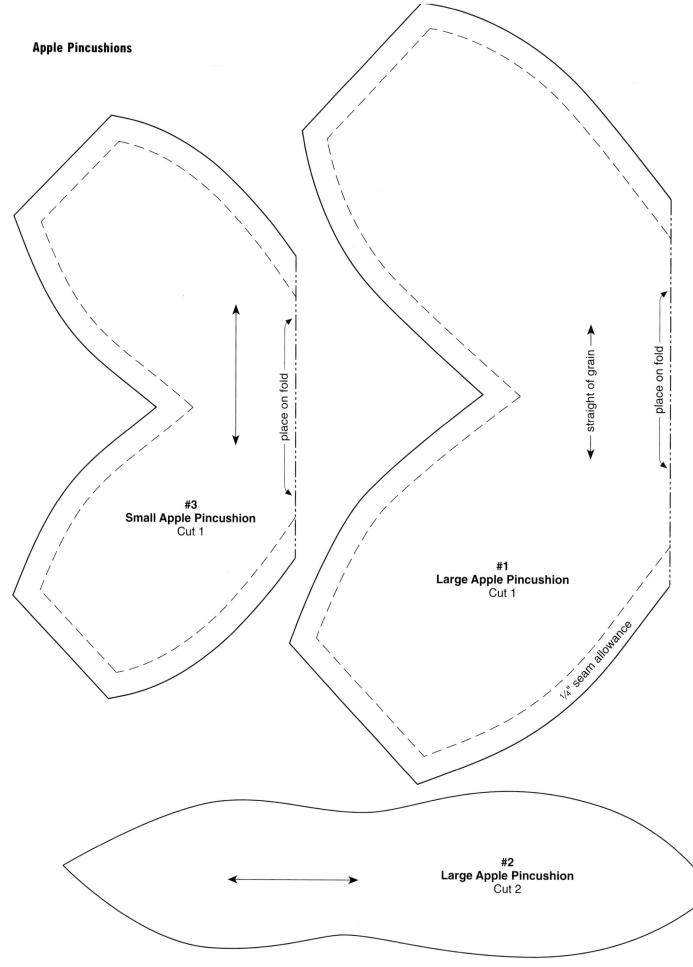

#3
Small Apple Pincushion
Cut 1

place on fold

#1
Large Apple Pincushion
Cut 1

straight of grain

place on fold

¼" seam allowance

#2
Large Apple Pincushion
Cut 2

QUILTMAKING BASICS

Equipment and Supplies

Scissors: a pair for cutting paper; a pair for cutting fabric; a small pointed pair for appliqué
Needles: size 7 embroidery; size 8 quilting or Betweens; size 11 Sharps for appliqué
#2 lead pencil
Mechanical pencil for marking quilting designs
White or yellow chalk pencil for marking appliqué pieces
Permanent marking pens for transferring embroidery designs and making quilt labels
Freezer paper (poly-coated)
Round toothpicks for turning appliqué seam allowances
Straight pins: glass head for piecing; $\frac{3}{4}$" sequin for hand appliqué
Quilters' press bars: made from flexible, heat-resistant nylon
Light box: helpful in making templates, but a window works fine
Paper-backed fusible web
Tear-away stabilizer
Quilting hoop or frame
$\frac{1}{4}$"-wide masking tape

Preparing Fabric

Use 100% cotton fabrics. Prewash them in warm water without detergent to prevent colors from running or bleeding when you launder the quilt later. Rinse the fabric until the water is clear. Dry, then press.

Yardage for the quilts in this book is based on quality cotton fabrics, 44" wide before prewashing. After washing and drying, we base cutting measurements on 42"-wide fabrics.

Machine Piecing

Maintaining an accurate $\frac{1}{4}$"-wide seam allowance throughout your piecing will yield the most successful results. Sew a pieced block and measure it to test the accuracy of your $\frac{1}{4}$" seam guide. After you have established an accurate $\frac{1}{4}$" seam guide, you are ready to piece.

1. Place right sides of pieces together, aligning the raw edges. Pin.
2. Set the stitch length at 12 stitches per inch. Stitch the pieces together, being careful not to tug or pull on the fabric as it is feeding through the machine.

Hand Piecing

Many quilters find hand piecing to be very relaxing. As with machine piecing, maintaining accurate $\frac{1}{4}$"-wide seams is important.

1. Place right sides of pieces together, matching the drawn seam lines. Pin.
2. Starting with a small backstitch, sew directly on the line using a small running stitch. Periodically, check to make sure you are stitching on the lines of both pieces and that you are leaving the seam allowances free. Finish with another small backstitch.

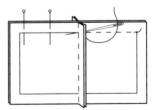

Making Half-Square Triangles

For perfect half-square triangle units, use preprinted grid paper. Squares and diagonal stitching lines are marked and they come in 1", $1\frac{1}{2}$", 2", $2\frac{1}{2}$", and 3" finished sizes. Follow the manufacturer's instructions for perfect machine-pieced squares with no marking and no waste.

1. Place the two selected fabrics right sides together; position the preprinted paper on the back side of the paper and pin in place.

2. Stitch on the diagonal lines, following the arrows. Cut apart on the vertical and horizontal lines and between the stitched seam lines.

3. Carefully remove the paper and press the seams toward the darker fabric.

Templates

Templates are used for hand and machine piecing as well as for appliqué. I make templates from template plastic for designs that will be used again and again. Use a sharp pencil or a fine-tip permanent pen to trace the lines.

Templates for Piecing

Here are two ways to mark and cut plastic templates for machine or hand piecing.

1. Mark the Sewing Line. This method is usually used for hand piecing but may also be used for machine piecing. Place the template plastic on top of the design. Trace the sewing line and cut the template on the line. Use a ruler to make straight lines when necessary. Mark the template number and the grain-line arrow on the template.

   To use the template, place it on the wrong side of the fabric, matching the grain-line arrow with the grain of the fabric. Trace around the template with a sharp pencil. Adding ¼"-wide seam allowances all around, cut out the pieces. Matching the drawn line, stitch the pieces together.

2. Mark the Cutting Line. This method is usually used for machine piecing. Place the template plastic on top of the design. Trace the cutting line and cut the template on the line. The seam lines are included. Mark the template number and the grain-line arrow on the template.

To use the template, place it on the wrong side of the fabric, matching the grain-line arrow with the grain of the fabric. Trace around the template with a sharp pencil. Cut out the pieces. With right sides together, stitch pieces, aligning the raw edges and allowing a ¼"-wide seam.

Note: *To cut reverse pieces, simply flip the template over, place it on the fabric, and trace.*

Templates for Appliqué

Place the template plastic on top of the design. Trace the lines and cut the template on the line. Do not add seam allowances to the templates. Mark the template number and grain-line arrow on the template.

Place the template face up on the right side of the fabric, matching the grain-line arrow with the grain of the fabric. Trace around the template with a lead pencil or chalk pencil. The drawn line establishes the turned-under stitching edge. Cut out the pieces, adding a scant ¼"-wide seam allowance all around. (A scant ¼"-wide seam allowance is ³⁄₁₆"–¼" wide or 2 fabric threads short of ¼".)

Freezer-Paper Templates

Poly-coated freezer paper is my favorite hand-appliqué template material. It doesn't move as you draw around it; therefore, your shapes are more accurate.

1. Place the freezer paper, shiny side down, on the design. Trace the motif with a lead pencil and cut it out on the line.

2. Place the shiny side of the freezer-paper piece on the right side of the fabric. Press with a hot iron for 10 to 15 seconds. Be sure to leave enough space between pieces for seam allowances.

3. Draw around the freezer-paper template with a white, yellow, or lead pencil.

4. Remove the freezer paper. Your template may be used three or more times.

5. Adding a scant ¼"-wide seam allowance, cut out the piece.

Appliqué Techniques

Hand Appliqué

I use two stitches when I appliqué by hand—the tack stitch and the ladder (blind) stitch.

Tack Stitch

My favorite appliqué stitch is the tack stitch, which was used frequently in the mid- to late-nineteenth century, especially in classic Baltimore Album quilts.

1. Pin the appliqué pieces in place on the background block, in the numerical order indicated on the templates.
2. Select a thread that matches the appliqué piece, not the background fabric. Tie a knot in an 18"-long single strand of thread.
3. Starting on the wrong side of the background fabric (the knot will be on the wrong side of the block), bring the needle up to the right side, just inside the turned edge of the appliqué piece, catching two or three threads. Pull the thread away from you, toward the background fabric, and insert the needle into the background fabric under the turned edge of the appliqué piece, directly next to the stitch you took in the appliqué piece. The stitch should be short and straight.

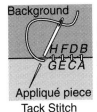

Note: The stitches are exaggerated for the purpose of illustration. The stitches should be practically invisible.

Tack Stitch

4. On the back side of the background fabric, turn the needle so it will come back up into the turned edge of the appliqué piece. Move the needle about 1/16" ahead, parallel to the edge of the appliqué piece. Bring the needle up into the appliqué piece, just as you did with the first stitch.
5. Roll under the seam allowance as you stitch the piece to the background. Use a round toothpick to turn the edge under about 1/2" at a time,

ahead of your stitching. Pull the stitches snugly but not so tightly that the piece puckers. Work from right to left if you are right-handed or left to right if you are left-handed.

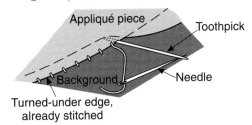

Roll under seam allowance with toothpick.

6. Continue stitching until you have gone all around the piece.
7. When you have finished appliquéing, take two small stitches on top of each other on the back side, at the end of the stitches.

Ladder (Blind) Stitch

The ladder stitch works well along straight edges and gentle curves. Switch to the tack stitch when you stitch inside points or tight outside points.

1. Pin the appliqué pieces in place on the background block, in the numerical order indicated on the templates.
2. Select a thread that matches the piece to be appliquéd, not the background fabric. Tie a knot in an 18"-long single strand of thread.
3. Starting on the wrong side of the background fabric, bring the needle up to the right side, just outside the turned edge of the appliqué piece. The knot will be on the wrong side of the block.
4. Make the first stitch by inserting the needle into the turned edge of the appliqué piece. Move the needle about 1/8" ahead, under the background fabric and parallel to the edge of the appliqué piece. Work from right to left if you are right-handed or left to right if you are left-handed.

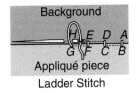

Ladder Stitch

5. Roll under the seam allowance as you stitch the piece to the background. Use a round toothpick to turn the edge under about ½" at a time, ahead of your stitching. (Refer to the illustration on page 85, top right.) Bring the needle up through the background fabric and into the turned edge of the appliqué piece. Pull the stitches snugly but not so tightly that the piece puckers.

6. Return the needle to the background fabric directly next to the point where the needle just came out of the appliqué piece. Then return the needle to the appliqué piece, just as you did in steps 4 and 5. Continue stitching until you have gone all around the piece.

7. When you have finished appliquéing, take two small stitches on top of each other on the back side, at the end of the stitches.

Tip

Curved shapes and inside corners are easier to turn under when the seam allowances are clipped up to, but not across, the turned edge.

Clips

Use your toothpick to turn under the edges at points.

2 Anchoring Stitches. Fold under and continue.

Do not turn under or appliqué any edges that will be covered by another appliqué piece. This reduces bulk and makes it easier to quilt your piece later.

Stems and Vines

Some of the quilts in this book require ¼"-wide (finished width) stems. I like to prepare lengths of bias-stem tubes at one time and then cut them into shorter lengths as I need them. Use quilters' press bars that are made from heat-resistant nylon instead of the metal ones.

Making Bias Stems and Vines

1. Fold the bottom left corner of a ½-yard piece of fabric to its opposite corner to create a right triangle. Crease the fabric on the fold. The resulting 45° crease will be used as a guide to cut strips along the true bias.

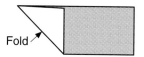

Fold

2. Cut strips 1¼" wide.

3. Fold the strips in half lengthwise, wrong sides together, and place the correct-size bias bar inside, next to the fold. Place the edge of the bias bar against the zipper foot. Stitch next to the bar, sliding the bar forward as you sew to keep the tube even. The distance from the fold to the stitching line should equal the finished stem width.

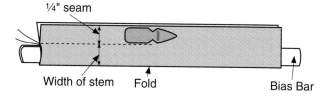

¼" seam

Width of stem   Fold   Bias Bar

4. With the bias bar still inside, trim the seam allowance to ⅛" wide.

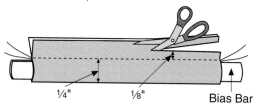

¼"   ⅛"   Bias Bar

5. With the seam centered in the back of the bias bar, press the tube. Remove the bar, then cut stems and vines into the lengths that you need.

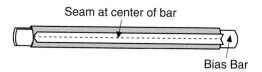

Seam at center of bar

Bias Bar

Appliquéing Stems and Vines

This is my favorite method for appliquéing finished bias strips.

To appliqué stems, vines, and basket handles:

Trace the stem-placement center line on the background fabric. Place the seam line of the stem on the placement line as shown. Using the tack appliqué stitch (page 85), stitch the stem to the background along both sides of the stem.

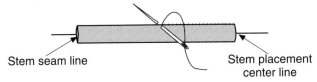

Stem seam line   Stem placement
                              center line

Machine Appliqué

I like to use a paper-backed fusible web to iron intricate designs to a background, then appliqué them with a machine zigzag stitch.

1. Place the template wrong side up on the paper side of fusible web (because the fusible web will be ironed onto the wrong side of the fabric).
2. Trace around the template with a lead pencil. For a reversed piece, flip the template over and trace around it.
3. Cut each piece from the fusible web, leaving a little extra outside the drawn lines.
4. Place the fusible-web piece on the wrong side of the fabric. Following manufacturer's instructions, iron in place.
5. Cut out the fabric piece on the drawn line. Remove the paper backing.
6. Place the appliqué piece on the background as indicated in the quilt plan. Fuse the piece in place with a hot iron.
7. Place tear-away stabilizer between the wrong side of the background block and the feed dog. Using a satin or buttonhole stitch, stitch around the appliqué piece. See illustrations below for stitches.

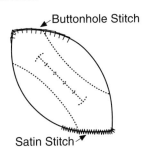

Buttonhole Stitch

Satin Stitch

8. Carefully remove tear-away stabilizer when you are done stitching.

Embroidery Stitches

Embroidery floss comes in skeins. A skein consists of six strands of floss. Carefully pull the end of the floss from the skein and cut an 18" length. Separate and pull out two strands, one at a time. Knot the strands together at the ends that have just been cut from the skein. Thread them on a size #7 embroidery needle.

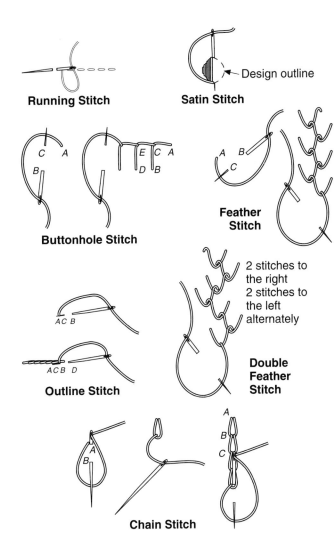

Running Stitch

Satin Stitch
Design outline

Buttonhole Stitch

Feather Stitch

Outline Stitch

2 stitches to the right
2 stitches to the left
alternately

Double Feather Stitch

Chain Stitch

Pressing

Pressing is an important aspect of quiltmaking at the piecing and appliqué stages, as well as when you add sashes and borders. Press carefully to avoid distorting the shapes.

- During piecing, press seam allowances to one side. Press toward the darker fabric, unless otherwise noted.
- For appliquéd blocks, place them wrong side up and press gently with a steam iron.
- Press all blocks, sashings, and borders before assembling the quilt top.
- Press the completed quilt top before quilting.

Adding Borders

Always measure first, before sewing borders to the quilt sides.

Straight-Cut Borders

I generally add the top and bottom borders first, then the side borders.

1. Measure the width of your quilt top through the center. Cut border strips to that measurement, piecing as necessary. Mark the centers of the border strips and the sides of the quilt top with pins. (The strips will be cut to the width required in each quilt plan.)

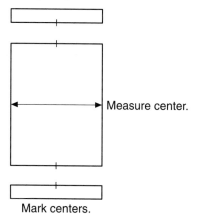

Measure center.

Mark centers.

2. With right sides together, pin the borders to the quilt top, matching the ends and the center marks and easing fullness as necessary.
3. Sew the border strips in place, using a $1/4$"-wide seam allowance.

4. Press seam allowances toward the border. See "Pressing" at left.
5. Measure the length of your quilt top through the center, including the border strips you just added. Cut border strips to that measurement, piecing as necessary. Mark the centers of the border strips and the sides of the quilt top with pins.

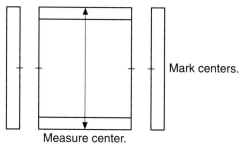

Mark centers.

Measure center.

6. With right sides together, pin the borders to the quilt top, matching the ends and the center marks and easing fullness as necessary.
7. Sew the border strips in place, using a $1/4$"- wide seam allowance. Press as you did with the top and bottom borders.

Mitered Borders

Estimate the finished outer dimensions of the quilt first, including borders. For example, if your quilt top measures $35^{1}/2$" x $50^{1}/2$" across the center and you want to add a 5"-wide finished border, your quilt should measure 45" x 60" after the borders are attached.

Cut the border strips to the finished dimensions plus at least $1/2$" for seam allowances. Add 2" for leeway, then trim the excess after completing the mitered corner.

Note: *If your quilt is to have multiple borders, sew the individual strips together and treat the resulting unit as a single border strip. This makes mitering corners easier and more accurate.*

1. Fold the quilt in half and mark the centers of all four sides with pins. Fold each border strip in half and mark the centers.

2. Measure the length and width of the quilt across the center. Note the measurements.

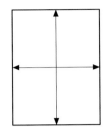

3. Place a pin at each end of the top and bottom border strips to mark the width of the quilt top. Repeat with the side borders.

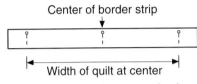

Center of border strip

Width of quilt at center

4. With right sides together, pin the borders to the quilt top, matching the ends and center marks and easing fullness as necessary. Border strips will extend beyond the edges of the quilt top.

5. Stitch, beginning and ending the stitching ¼" from the raw edges of the quilt top. Repeat with the remaining borders.

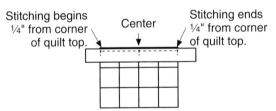

Stitching begins ¼" from corner of quilt top.

Center

Stitching ends ¼" from corner of quilt top.

6. Working at the ironing board, fold under one border strip at a 45° angle and adjust so seam lines match. Press fold to crease and pin border strips near the creased line.

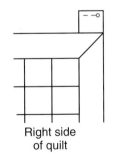

Right side of quilt

7. On the wrong side of the quilt, machine stitch on the creased line. Sew from the inside corner to the outside edge. Press seam open and trim away excess border fabric. Repeat with the remaining corners.

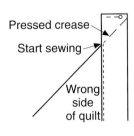

Pressed crease

Start sewing

Wrong side of quilt

Quilt Finishing

Marking the Quilting Design

Quilting adds wonderful depth and dimension to your quilt. Quilting can enhance certain designs created in your piecing and appliqué or can be used to counterbalance certain design elements. For instance, quilting curved designs within a Log Cabin block can soften or "round" the straight lines of the logs.

Make up your own quilting designs or use precut quilting stencils that come in many designs and sizes. If you plan to quilt "in-the-ditch," there is no need to mark quilting lines. If you decide to outline quilt a uniform distance from seam lines, either mark your lines "by eye" or use ¼"-wide masking tape to establish the lines. Do not leave tape on a quilt overnight; the residue may be difficult to remove.

More complex quilting patterns should be marked on a quilt top before it is layered with batting and backing. Always press the finished quilt top before marking. To mark quilting lines, use a hard lead pencil (#3 or #4) on light fabrics; for dark fabrics, use a fine-line chalk marker or a silver pencil. Before marking the quilt, test to make sure that the markings can be removed.

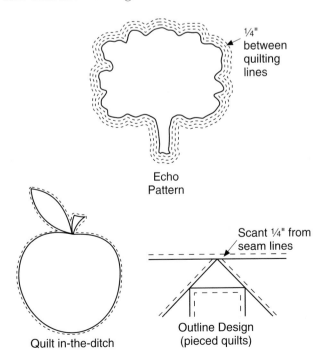

¼" between quilting lines

Echo Pattern

Scant ¼" from seam lines

Quilt in-the-ditch

Outline Design (pieced quilts)

Backing

The backing should extend at least 2" beyond all sides. I cut all quilt backs from the lengthwise grain line of the fabric because the quilts remain straighter after laundering. Depending on the width of the quilt, sew two or three lengths of fabric together. Cut the second length in half lengthwise, trim away the selvages, and piece it to each side of the center width as shown.

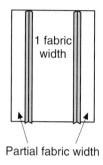

Partial fabric width

Batting

Select your batting after you have decided how the quilt will be used. Thick battings are usually used for tied bed quilts. Low-loft batting is also used for bed quilts. Thinner battings are easier to quilt and work well for wall and table quilts.

The batting should extend at least 2" beyond all sides of the quilt top.

Layering the Quilt

1. Lay the backing, wrong side up, on a large flat surface. Tape the corners in place.
2. Lay the batting on top of the backing. Smooth out any wrinkles and be sure the batting extends evenly on all edges of the batting.
3. Place quilt top, right side up, on top of the batting, aligning corners. Smooth out any wrinkles.

---

4. Baste the layers together. For quilts that will be hand quilted, baste all three layers together, using a large needle and quilting thread. Basting lines should radiate from the center.

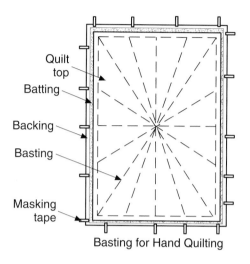

Basting for Hand Quilting

For quilts that will be machine quilted, baste the layers with #2 rustproof safety pins. Place the pins 4" apart.

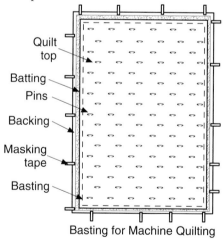

Basting for Machine Quilting

5. Trim batting and backing to within 1" of the quilt-top edges.

Tip

Choose a hoop that is comfortable for you to handle and at least 14" in diameter.

Tip

Use the smallest needle that you can comfortably handle; the smaller the needle, the smaller your stitches will be.

Binding

Bindings can be made from straight-cut or bias-cut strips of fabric.

Straight-Cut Binding

1. Measure the width of your quilt in the same manner as you did for the borders. Cut strips long enough to match that measurement for each side. Cut the strips as wide as specified for the quilt.
2. Mark the centers of the quilt top on all sides. Mark the center of the binding strips. With right sides together, pin the binding strips to the top and bottom sides, matching the raw edges of the binding with the raw edges of the quilt top. Also match the center marks and be sure the ends of the binding strips are flush with the edges of the quilt top.

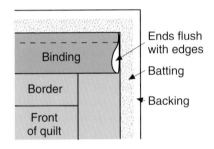

3. Sew the binding strips in place, using a ¼"-wide seam allowance.
4. Trim the batting and backing even with the quilt top.
5. Fold the binding to the back side of the quilt. Turn under the seam allowance and blindstitch in place.

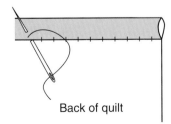

6. Next add the side bindings. Measure the length of your quilt, including the binding strips you

just added. Cut the remaining binding strips to that measurement plus 3". Pin the binding to the sides of the quilt, matching the center marks and the raw edges of the binding with the raw edges of the quilt top. The binding will extend 1½" at each end.

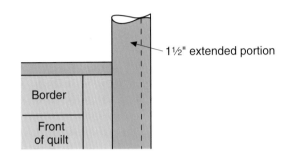

7. Trim the batting and backing even with the edges of the quilt top.
8. Fold the extended portion of the binding down onto the binding so that the folded edges are flush with the edges of the top and bottom binding.
9. Stitch through all layers next to the previous stitching.

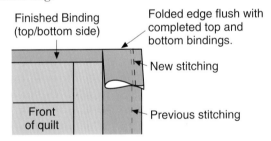

10. Fold the binding to the back side of the quilt. Turn under the seam allowance and blindstitch in place.

Bias Binding

To cut bias binding:
1. Fold over a corner of the fabric on the diagonal.

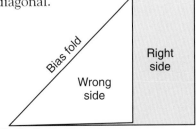

2. Cut along the diagonal fold.
3. Cut bias strips 2½" wide, parallel to the first diagonal cut as shown.

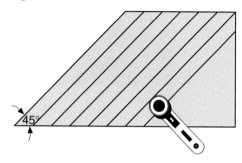

4. Trim the strip ends at a 45° angle and piece the ends to make a continuous strip the length required for the quilt. Press the seams open.

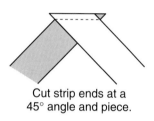

Cut strip ends at a 45° angle and piece.

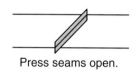

Press seams open.

To attach bias binding:

1. Measure around the outside edge of your quilt and add 10". Cut bias binding, following the steps above.
2. Fold the binding strip in half lengthwise, wrong sides together, and press.

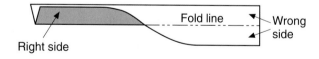

3. Unfold the binding at one end and turn under ¼" at a 45° angle as shown and press.

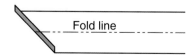

4. Starting in the center of one side, align the raw edges of the binding with the raw edge of the quilt top; pin in place.

5. Leave a 2" starting tail and, using a ¼"-wide seam allowance, stitch through all layers. Stop stitching ¼" from the corner and backstitch.

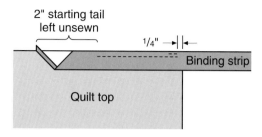

6. Reposition the quilt to begin stitching along the next side. Fold the binding away from the quilt as shown, then fold again (creating a pleat at the corner) to place binding along the second edge of the quilt. Begin stitching at the edge and continue to the next corner, stopping ¼" from the corner and backstitch.

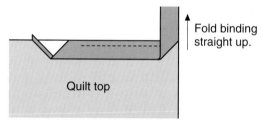

7. Repeat the stitching and mitering process on the remaining sides and corners.
8. After turning the fourth corner, stitch to within a few inches of the starting tail. Stop stitching. Tuck the ending tail inside the starting tail. Trim the ending tail to 1".

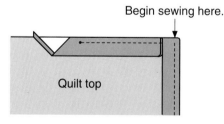

9. With the end of the binding tucked inside the starting tail, align the raw edges of the quilt; stitch in place.

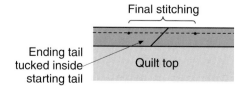

10. Trim excess batting and backing even with the edge of the quilt top.
11. Turn the binding to the back of the quilt. Turn under the seam allowance and blindstitch in place. At each corner, fold the binding as shown to form mitered corners on the back of the quilt.

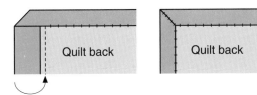

Quilt Labels

Just imagine your great-grandchildren finding some of your quilts in storage some day after you are gone. The quilts are exquisite, but there are no labels on them so they have no idea that the quilts were made by you or a group of your friends. It is a good idea to label a quilt with its name, the name and address of its maker, and the date that it was completed. Also include the quilter's name if the quilt was quilted by someone other than the one who pieced or appliquéd it.

Use a permanent marking pen to print or write all of this information on a piece of muslin. (Or, hand- or machine-embroider the information!) Press the raw edges to the wrong side of the label and stitch it to the lower corner of the quilt, being careful that the stitches do not show on the front side of the quilt.

PILLOW FINISHING

Unless otherwise noted, use ¼"-wide seam allowances.

Knife-Edge Pillow

1. Place the pillow top and backing with right sides together. Begin stitching 1" from a corner and continue stitching around all four corners. Stop stitching 1" inside the last corner as shown.

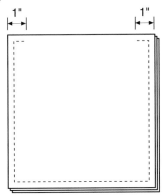

2. Turn right side out through the opening. Insert pillow form. If you like, fill in the corners with some batting. This keeps the corners plump.
3. Turn under the seam allowance and blindstitch the opening closed.

Corded-Edge Pillow

1. Measure all around the sides of the pillow top and cut ¼" cording to that measurement plus 4". Cut and piece 1½"-wide bias strips to make the same length as the cording. See directions on page 86 for cutting and piecing bias strips.
2. Fold the bias strip over the cording, wrong sides together, aligning the raw edges. Use a zipper foot to stitch closely to the cording so that the fabric encases the cording snugly.

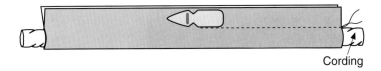

Cording

3. With right sides together, match the raw edges of the cording with the raw edges of the pillow top. Beginning at the center of one side and leaving a 1" starting tail, machine baste the cording to the pillow top. Begin at the center of one side. Stop stitching about 1" from where the two ends will be joined.

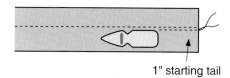

1" starting tail

4. To turn square corners, clip into the cording seam allowance.

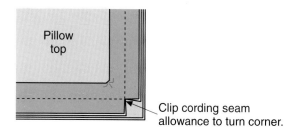

Pillow top

Clip cording seam allowance to turn corner.

5. To join the ends, remove a few stitches to open up the bias covering. Trim the cording so the ends meet as shown. Sew the ends of the cording together by hand. Turn under the end of the starting-tail bias covering. Trim ending-tail bias covering and lay it on top of starting tail.

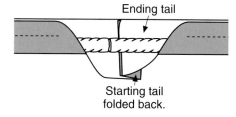

Ending tail

Starting tail folded back.

6. Refold bias covering to complete the basting.

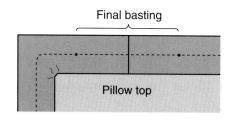

Final basting

Pillow top

7. Finish by following steps 1–3 for the knife-edge pillow on page 93.

Ruffled-Edge Pillow

1. Cut 2 ruffle strips, each 7" x 42". Stitch the ends of the strips together to form a 7" x 84" circle. With wrong sides together, fold the 7" strip in half lengthwise and press.

2. Machine stitch two rows of basting stitches all around the circle, $1/8$" and $1/4$" from the raw edge. Gather by pulling the bobbin threads of each stitching line, working from each end to the center. Stop gathering when the circle measures just over 50".

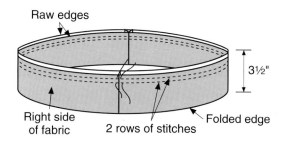

Raw edges

3½"

Right side of fabric

2 rows of stitches

Folded edge

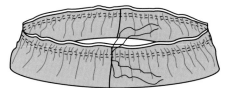

Pull bobbin threads to gather.

3. With right sides together, place the ruffle on the pillow top, aligning the raw edges. Distribute the gathers evenly so that there is a little more fullness around the corners. Machine baste in place, $1/4$" from edge.

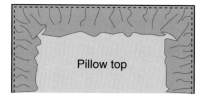

Pillow top

4. Finish by following steps 1–3 for the knife-edge pillow on page 93.

ABOUT THE AUTHOR

The quilting world has been a large part of Laurene Sinema's life since 1978, when she and her friend, Janet Carruth, founded the Arizona Quilters Guild. They opened The Quilted Apple a few months later and in 1987 founded the Arizona Quilt Project. Laurene served as president of both organizations and in 1983 became sole owner of The Quilted Apple.

Sharing fine hand-appliqué techniques and folk-art designs in classes at The Quilted Apple, International Quilt Festival and symposiums around the nation gives Laurene much pleasure. She is well known for the quilting stories she tells during her classes and writes in her books.

A designer, author, lecturer, teacher, mother and grand-mother, Laurene lives in Phoenix, Arizona, with her husband, Gerry. Visitors often see Gerry at The Quilted Apple — he calls himself "resident janitor." The Sinemas have five children, twenty-one grandchildren and one great-grand-child. It is Laurene's theory that a family so large must keep one "young!"

Other books by this author are *Appliqué! Appliqué!! Appliqué!!!* (1992); *Primitive Folk Art Designs from Antique Album Quilts* (1990); and *A Bushel of Apples* with Janet Carruth (1981).

RESOURCES

The products listed may be available in your favorite quilt shop. If you are unable to find them, we offer a mail-order service.

Rug hooking supplies, wools, and hand-dyed wools

Books
   Appliqué! Appliqué!! Appliqué!!!
   *Primitive Folk Art Designs from Antique
      Album Quilts*
   A Bushel of Apples

Call or write for more information and prices:
   The Quilted Apple
   3043 North 24th Street
   Phoenix, AZ 85016
   (602) 956-0904

That Patchwork Place Publications and Products

BOOKS

All the Blocks Are Geese by Mary Sue Suit
Angle Antics by Mary Hickey
Animas Quilts by Jackie Robinson
Appliqué Borders: An Added Grace by Jeana Kimball
Appliquilt: Whimsical One-Step Appliqué by Tonee White
Baltimore Bouquets by Mimi Dietrich
Basket Garden by Mary Hickey
Biblical Blocks by Rosemary Makhan
Blockbuster Quilts by Margaret J. Miller
Botanical Wreaths by Laura M. Reinstatler
Calendar Quilts by Joan Hanson
Cathedral Window: A Fresh Look by Nancy J. Martin
The Cat's Meow by Janet Kime
Colourwash Quilts by Deirdre Amsden
Corners in the Cabin by Paulette Peters
Country Medallion Sampler by Carol Doak
Country Threads by Connie Tesene and Mary Tendall
Easy Machine Paper Piecing by Carol Doak
Easy Quilts...By Jupiter!® by Mary Beth Maison
Even More by Trudie Hughes
Fantasy Flowers by Doreen Cronkite Burbank
Fit To Be Tied by Judy Hopkins
Five- and Seven-Patch Blocks & Quilts for the ScrapSaver by Judy Hopkins
Four-Patch Blocks & Quilts for the ScrapSaver by Judy Hopkins
Fun with Fat Quarters by Nancy J. Martin
Go Wild with Quilts by Margaret Rolfe
Handmade Quilts by Mimi Dietrich
Happy Endings by Mimi Dietrich
The Heirloom Quilt by Yolande Filson and Roberta Przybylski
Holiday Happenings by Christal Carter
Home for Christmas by Nancy J. Martin and Sharon Stanley
In The Beginning by Sharon Evans Yenter
Irma's Sampler by Irma Eskes
Jacket Jazz by Judy Murrah
Lessons in Machine Piecing by Marsha McCloskey
Little By Little: Quilts in Miniature by Mary Hickey
Little Quilts by Alice Berg, Sylvia Johnson, and Mary Ellen Von Holt
Lively Little Logs by Donna McConnell
Loving Stitches by Jeana Kimball
Make Room for Quilts by Nancy J. Martin
More Template-Free® *Quiltmaking* by Trudie Hughes
Nifty Ninepatches by Carolann M. Palmer
Nine-Patch Blocks & Quilts for the ScrapSaver by Judy Hopkins
Not Just Quilts by Jo Parrott
Oh! Christmas Trees compiled by Barbara Weiland

On to Square Two by Marsha McCloskey
Osage County Quilt Factory by Virginia Robertson
Painless Borders by Sally Schneider
A Perfect Match by Donna Lynn Thomas
Picture Perfect Patchwork by Naomi Norman
Piecemakers® *Country Store* by the Piecemakers
Pineapple Passion by Nancy Smith and Lynda Milligan
A Pioneer Doll and Her Quilts by Mary Hickey
Pioneer Storybook Quilts by Mary Hickey
Prairie People—Cloth Dolls to Make and Cherish by Marji Hadley and J. Dianne Ridgley
Quick & Easy Quiltmaking by Mary Hickey, Nancy J. Martin, Marsha McCloskey and Sara Nephew
The Quilted Apple by Laurene Sinema
Quilted for Christmas compiled by Ursula Reikes
The Quilters' Companion compiled by That Patchwork Place
The Quilting Bee by Jackie Wolff and Lori Aluna
Quilts for All Seasons by Christal Carter
Quilts for Baby: Easy as A, B, C by Ursula Reikes
Quilts for Kids by Carolann M. Palmer
Quilts from Nature by Joan Colvin
Quilts to Share by Janet Kime
Red and Green: An Appliqué Tradition by Jeana Kimball
Red Wagon Originals by Gerry Kimmel and Linda Brannock
Rotary Riot by Judy Hopkins and Nancy J. Martin
Rotary Roundup by Judy Hopkins and Nancy J. Martin
Round About Quilts by J. Michelle Watts
Samplings from the Sea by Rosemary Makhan
Scrap Happy by Sally Schneider
ScrapMania by Sally Schneider
Sensational Settings by Joan Hanson
Sewing on the Line by Lesly-Claire Greenberg
Shortcuts: A Concise Guide to Rotary Cutting by Donna Lynn Thomas (metric version available)
Shortcuts Sampler by Roxanne Carter
Shortcuts to the Top by Donna Lynn Thomas
Small Talk by Donna Lynn Thomas
Smoothstitch™ *Quilts* by Roxi Eppler
The Stitchin' Post by Jean Wells and Lawry Thorn
Strips That Sizzle by Margaret J. Miller
Sunbonnet Sue All Through the Year by Sue Linker
Tea Party Time by Nancy J. Martin
Template-Free® *Quiltmaking* by Trudie Hughes
Template-Free® *Quilts and Borders* by Trudie Hughes
Template-Free® *Stars* by Jo Parrott
Two for Your Money by Jo Parrott
Watercolor Quilts by Pat Magaret and Donna Slusser
Women and Their Quilts by Nancyann Johanson Twelker

TOOLS

4" Baby Bias Square®   BiRangle™   Ruby Beholder™
6" Bias Square®   Pineapple Rule   ScrapMaster
8" Bias Square®   Rotary Mate™
Metric Bias Square®   Rotary Rule™

VIDEO

Shortcuts to America's Best-Loved Quilts™

Many titles are available at your local quilt shop. For more information, send $2 for a color catalog to That Patchwork Place, Inc., PO Box 118, Bothell WA 98041-0118 USA.

☎ Call 1-800-426-3126 for the name and location of the quilt shop nearest you.